Men CONQUERING Depression

Men
CONQUERING
Depression

Empowering Journeys Towards Resilience
and Renewal

Fred F. Majette Jr.

Men Conquering Depression

To my father, Yahuwah, whose unwavering presence, and boundless grace has guided me through the darkest moments and illuminated the path towards healing.

To my loving wife, whose support, patience, and encouragement have been my anchor. Your belief in me inspires every word written in this book.

To my children, Quimari & Christina, returning to you was the purpose of my journey. This book is a testament that we can overcome anything. You are my greatest joy and my endless motivation.

In a world where strength is praised,

Where men conquer mountains, unafraid,

There lies a book, a guide sincere,

To help men conquer their inner fear.

"Men Conquering Depression" it's called,

A beacon of hope for the weary and appalled,

With words of wisdom, compassion, and grace, it

offers solace in life's darkest space.

Open its page, let your heart unfold,

Find understanding, let your story be told,

For within these words, you'll find a friend, A

companion on the journey to mend.

Through every chapter, you'll discover light,

Guiding you through the shadows of night,

With empathy and courage, it will inspire,

To conquer the demons that dwell in the mire.

So, dive into this book, let its words embrace,

And let it guide you to a better place,

For "Men Conquering Depression," is here to

remind you that help is always near.

May these words welcome you on this quest, to find healing, strength, and be your best,

Embrace the words, let them be your guide, as

you conquer the darkness deep inside.

FM

Contents

Introduction:
The World of Whispers and Silence   10

Chapters

1. Coming Out of the Darkness   16
2. Get Out, Get Help   40
3. The Stress of it All   55
4. Removing a Failure Mindset   62
5. When There's A Chink in my Armor   76

6. Going from Brokenness to Wholeness   96
7. Removing shame and Guilt   135
8. There Is Hope   145
9. Accountability and Responsibility   147
10. Restart, Renew and Restore   161

Acknowledgement	170
Epilogue	172
Appendix	175
Author Bio	178

Men CONQUERING Depression

INTRODUCTION
The World of Whispers and Silence

In a world full of whispers and silence, there's something often seen, yet without reliance. It is the truth and struggle of man that hides behind veiled words, and societal acceptance. A presence acknowledged, but rarely heard.

It's the weight of his burdens carried with grace yet etched on his face and reflected in his pace. The invisible battles were fought day and night. A struggle endured, concealed from sight. It's an unspoken pain that lingers within him, woven in stories where his struggles begin. The scars that mark a journey unseen and a testament to strength though not foreseen.

It's the loneliness he feels in a crowded room. The silent tears that fall in the gloom. The weariness that shadows his weary eyes, whispering a silent plea for understanding lies. His dreams and hopes are kept close to his heart along with the unvoiced desires awaiting their start. The fears and doubts that hold him back are unspoken truths that keep his heart intact.

So, let's remember, in our daily strife sometimes the most visible battles in life are the ones left unspoken, yet deeply felt. A kind word or gesture can help his heart melt. Let's strive to be mindful, empathetic, and kind; to see the unseen and truly unwind. For though it's not spoken, it's there to see. The invisible struggles that will make him truly free.

We live in a world that often places unrealistic expectations on men to be strong, invulnerable, and emotionally detached. Therefore, the topic of depression among men remains a largely unspoken and a misunderstood issue. We see the effects of it. The violence towards others especially women, the drug abuse, the lack of accountability and the strain upon our community. With this in mind, we should be able to see that it is crucial to recognize that men, just like anyone else, can experience the depths of depression. "Men Conquering Depression" is a book that aims to shine a light on the unique challenges men face when dealing with this mental health condition.

Unfortunately, depression knows no boundaries and will affect any man from any background. However, it is essential to say that men experience depression very differently due to societal and cultural norms even biological factors. Men often internalize their emotions, fearing that expressing vulnerability will undermine their masculinity. This societal pressure can lead to avoidance, self-isolation, and an inability to seek help. "Men Conquering Depression," seeks to break down these barriers by providing a safe space for men to understand and address their mental health struggles.

Understanding Male Depression

Within these pages we dive into the intricacies of male depression, exploring the signs, symptoms, and risk factors specifically to men. By understanding the nuances of depression in men, we can begin dismantling the stereotypes and misconceptions that surround this condition. Though personal narratives and informative data about depression, readers will gain insight into the unique challenges men face when struggling with depression.

We explore the societal and cultural factors that contribute to the stigma surrounding male depression. Men are expected to be stoic, strong, and unyielding, making it difficult for them to express their emotions openly. By delving into these expectations, we aim to create a space for them to challenge societal norms and redefine masculinity in a way that embraces emotional well-being and vulnerability.

One of the most significant obstacles men face when dealing with depression is the stigma surrounding their mental health. Society often expects men to be self-reliant and dismissive of their own emotional struggles. "Men Conquering Depression," addresses the importance of challenging societal norms and encourage men to seek the help they need without fear or shame.

Through personal anecdotes and empowering stores of men who have triumphed over their depression, we aim to inspire a shift in attitudes towards entail health and promote a culture of openness and acceptance.

We give practical advice on how to decide when professional help is needed and offer guidance on navigating the mental health system. By destigmatizing helping seeking behaviors, we hope to empower men to take charge of their mental well -being.

Strategies for Conquering Depression

In the ten chapters of "Men Conquering Depression," we delve into practical strategies and techniques that men can employ to overcome their depression. From evidence-based therapies to self-care practices. Within this book we offer a toolkit for men to develop resilience, foster emotional wellbeing, and regain control over their lives.

We explore various therapeutic approaches, such as cognitive-behavioral therapy, mindfulness practices, and support groups, that have proven effective in treating depression. Additionally, we emphasize the importance of self-care activities, such as exercise, healthy eating, and engaging in hobbies, as essential components of a comprehensive treatment plan.

"Men Conquering Depression" is a book that seeks to provide men with the knowledge, resources and support they need to navigate their journey towards conquering depression. By addressing the unique challenges men face, challenging societal norms, and providing practical strategies, this book aims to empower men to take control of their mental health and find a path towards healing and resilience.

It is our hope that through the insights shared in this book, men will feel validated in their experiences, encouraged to seek help without shame, and inspired to redefine masculinity in a way that embraces emotional well-being. Together, we can create a society where men feel empowered to conquer their depression and live fulfilling lives. Let "Men Conquering Depression" be your guide on this transformative journey.

Emerge into the Light

A Journey of Hope and Healing

Chapter 1

Coming Out of the Darkness

"Like stars emerging from the night, men have the power to rise above the darkness and illuminate the world with their strength, courage and resilience."

Before we get into the beginning of this journey, let's get one of the biggest lies told by any man ever out of the way. Question: How are you doing guys? The typical answer by us men is usually, I'm ok, I'm good and I'm alright. They are all Lies!

The sad part about this is we will go throughout our lives saying this same lie repeatedly. When does this end? When can we finally speak our truth? The honest answer is no…I am not ok.

Boys Don't Cry

The saying that *"boys don't cry"* has long been engrained in our society, perpetuating harmful gender stereotypes, and inhibiting emotional expressions in males. This has long been the ideal reference to men and their emotions. What happens to the tears that are not allowed to flow? These tears turn into a deeply hidden untamed ocean of emotions. Years of this unhealthy routine create a dark place within us men. This learned behavior has been reinforced through the lives of many young men. It has contributed to the suppression of the emotions in males.

Understanding the historical context helps us recognize the need for change. Emotional suppression can have detrimental effects on mental health by discouraging emotional expression and their voices, we deny men the opportunity to own their feelings, leading to unresolved emotions, increased stress levels and a higher likelihood of developing mental health issues. Encourage emotional expression for us men so we can have essential overall well-being.

The saying that *"boys don't cry"* is rooted in toxic masculinity, which promotes the idea that showing vulnerability is a sign of weakness. This perpetuates an unhealthy and unrealistic expectation for men to constantly display strength and stoicism. By challenging this notion, we can redefine masculinity to include emotional intelligence and vulnerability.

Embracing emotional expression in boys fosters empathy and understanding to express their emotions. They develop a greater ability for empathy which is vital for building healthy relationships and promoting equality between genders. Challenging the cycle of emotional suppression teaches boys that it is acceptable to cry and express their emotions which helps create a more compassionate and inclusive society. It allows them to develop healthy coping mechanisms, communicate more effectively and seek support when needed.

Positive role models and education on this topic play a crucial part and challenges the *"boys don't cry"* theory by encouraging a man's sensitive side to flow instead of being ignored. Schools, families, and communities should promote positive male role models who are emotionally expressive. By providing education on emotional intelligence a promoting open dialogue, we can create a supportive environment for boys to express their feelings.

This saying should be changed to boys should cry. It is ok for boys to express their sadness and grief. Encouraging boys to express their emotions at a younger age not only improves their mental well-being as adults but also promotes empathy, equality, and healthier relationships. It is time to redefine masculinity and break free from restrictive gender norms. This allows boys and men to embrace their emotions without fear. Otherwise, we will continue to see the constant testimonials of men who are emotionally dysfunctional.

The Origin of the Dark Place

Our minds occupy the core of our emotional dark places. The results of common cognitive biases within men are invisible because the first victim is our thinking process. Depression attacks the way we think and feel which can be invisible to everyone including ourselves. It starts to distort how we view certain situations. Minor matters could become more extreme and more difficult to figure out. Our thought patterns begin to change from a normal complex system to a more black or white simplistic system. For example, some men suffering from depression may perceive themselves or their circumstance as either perfect or completely flawed, without acknowledging any middle ground.

We start overgeneralizing all negative events. Men may begin to view all negative events as representations of a pattern of failure that will always continue to end the same way in the future. We begin to selectively focus on negative specs of a situation while ignoring or discounting any positive elements. We tend to magnify our failures and shortcomings by filtering out all events that have occurred in our lives. We inwardly react and respond.

While we are personalizing, we are also over exaggerating scenarios in our lives. Further fueling our feelings of despair and helplessness. Within this type of thinking, we will begin to base our beliefs and judgments solely on our emotions without considering objective evidence. We believe that though we feel a certain way it is evident of our truth therefore disregarding any contradictory evidence.

Types of Depression

There are several types of depression that can bring a man to a dark place mentally but the two most common are clinical depressions such as Major Depressive Disorder, MDD and Persistent Depressive Disorder, PDD.

These conditions can have severe symptoms that affect an individual's mental well-being and overall outlook on life.

Major depressive disorder is a mental health condition characterized by persistent feelings of sadness, hopelessness and a loss of interest or pleasure and activities. It may also involve significant changes in appetite, weight loss or gain, difficulty concentrating or making decisions, fatigue or loss of energy, disturbances in sleep like insomnia, restlessness or slow moving, guilt and recurrent thoughts of death and suicide. The more serious the symptoms get the quicker you should be seeking professional help.

A MDD diagnosis usually involves symptoms to be present for at least two weeks and significantly interfere with daily functioning and well-being. It is important to note that MDD is different from normal feelings of sadness or grief. It is a lot more intense with more persistent emotions. MDD can occur at any age and can be triggered by a combination of genetic, biological, environmental, and psychological factors. It is a common mental health condition affecting millions of men worldwide.

Treatment for MDD often involves a combination of therapies including psychotherapy and medication. Psychotherapy, also known as cognitive behavioral therapy, can help individuals find and remove negative thought patterns and behaviors that contribute to depression. Man to man, if you know of someone experiencing symptoms of MDD, it is important to help them seek help from a mental health professional. They can provide an accurate diagnosis and develop a personalized treatment plan to help you manage and alleviate the symptoms of MDD. Remember with proper support and treatment men living with MDD can experience improvement in their mood and overall well-being.

Though MDD is the most common form of depression, PDD, Persistent Depressive Disorder is also known as dysthymia. Dysthymia has similar characteristics and episodes of severe depressive symptoms like MDD but the symptoms last longer. PDD involves a persistent low mood that can persist for years. Key characteristics of PDD is the chronic nature of the symptoms. While the intensity of the symptoms may fluctuate over time individuals with PDD often experience a provocative sense of sadness and dissatisfaction that persists for an extended period, significantly impacting their daily functioning and quality of life. It is also important to note that PDD can coexist with other mental health conditions, such as anxiety disorders and may require a comprehensive treatment approach.

Untreated Depression on Society

It is fair to say that most crimes are committed by men who are suffering from some sought of depression that has been untreated, unseen, or ignored. They live in a complete imbalance of emotions. While the onset of depression itself does not inherently lead to criminal behavior, it can contribute to certain risk factors and circumstances that may increase the likelihood of criminal involvement.

Depression can impair decision making skills and increase impulsive behaviors. This symptom can cause men to engage in criminal acts without fully considering the consequences. Family and friends may notice them interacting with substance abuse which can lower their inhibitions, increase their aggression, and contribute to their criminal behavior.

There is also a socioeconomic factor of depression. Depression can be associated with lower socioeconomic status, therefore limiting access to resources, including higher levels of stress among men. These factors can always increase the risk of criminal involvement.

Men may resort to illegal activities to meet their basic needs or alleviate their distress. With some men, as they struggle with depression, they choose to abandon what is familiar to them and choose isolation as a way of escape. This is connected to an all or nothing perspective due to depression. Men in this position feel as if abandoning their families, their careers and everything they worked hard to achieve will relieve their minds of the constant reminder of their failure. This further emphasize the importance of early detection among men suffering from depression. Impulsive acts such as abandonment are not only associated with depression but also with antisocial personality disorders and contact disorders which are also associated with criminal behavior.

Elements of Depression Old and New

Men experiencing depression may also feel deep loneliness. There are reports of a male loneliness epidemic on the rise, but this can be due to societal pressures on men. As men we either internalize our feelings or we show them in a violative way.

The younger men who experience the symptoms of depression show signs within their adolescence. The early onset of abusive environments for male children compounded with societal pressures detach from their emotions as they grow into manhood. It is a recipe for a troubled adult man who passes his trauma on to the next generation.

 We see it daily on the news how groups of young men act out in society whether violently towards each other or toward innocent bystanders. The world sees them as menaces, but it is a lot deeper than that. No one takes the time to find the root of the disease. Society's answer is always to imprison it not to treat the problem. The way some parts of the world handle this home-grown monstrosity is a testament to its inability to provide or have real concern about its mental illness situation.

There are so many stresses connected to men and depression. One main stressor for men living with depression is divorce. Divorce can have a significant impact on a man's mental health which can lead to depression. It is often accompanied by a range of intense emotions including sadness, anger, and guilt but there is also a silent fear that no man willingly talks about. We men struggle to process these emotions that may feel overwhelming by the loss of their marriage and the changes it brings. This emotional turmoil can contribute to depression within men.

Men along with women deal with loss of identity when confronted with divorce. True fathers and husbands are proud of their roles within their families and the possibility of losing their position would disrupt our entire lives. The breakdown of our family can leave us questioning our own self-worth which causes our self-esteem to plummet.

Depression itself has its own challenges but adding financial stress along with it can contribute to mental hardship. Financial challenges, such as separating assets spousal support, and child support payments can leave a man feeling depleted. Men feel the burden of these financial obligations which led to stress, anxiety, and a sense of uncertainty about their future which can lead to depression. Men can experience feelings of loss and grief in the sense of disconnection from their children.

Separation can create extreme hardship and contribute to depressive symptoms.

Society views a man as not having the ability to connect with his children as a mother does however, that is not true at all. Fathers can express and feel their own parental connection to their children even as the woman carries the child within her womb. The trauma connected with losing your child due to divorce can result in the man experiencing bitterness. This can create anger in a man reducing him to acting out on the mother for purposely destroying his family.

For many men being a father is a central aspect of their identity and a source of pride. Losing custody can result in the loss of a significant part of their identity and cause them to suffer inside. They may question their abilities as a parent, their value in their children's lives, and their overall self-esteem.

Divorces that end bitterly usually involve children used as pawns to hurt one another. Most of the time the court system allows the children to stay with the mother, not even considering the father's vital role in their life. In these situations, the father begins to feel as if his only role in his children's lives is to hand over money, otherwise, he is of no value.

I have counseled many men who fear losing time with their children because of a bitter divorce. They all expressed feelings of anxiety, frustration, and depression. Those of us who have strong bonds with our children begin to feel a significant void when we lose custody of our children. We lose the daily joyful interactions, the shared activities, and their ability to be actively involved in their children's lives. This can be emotionally draining and stressful for men.

Men may face challenges by proving their suitability as a parent after divorce which they never had to do prior. All this happens while meeting with lawyers, court dates, changing addresses, and possible charges brought against you. Living in this world wind of emotions, divorce can catapult a man into depression. This prolonged period of stress and uncertainty can take a toll on their mental health. Most of us will not express these emotions of fear of seeming weak. The reality of not waking up to our family anymore can create stress that is overwhelming.

Why does the Silence Continue?

Society gender roles are part of the problems men face today. We live under an unspoken, uncompromising rule that has been heavily enforced which we all must abide by. Unfortunately, men have implemented these unwritten rules themselves. Men of the past created the roles and mentality of men to separate us from women. They were completely unaware of the emotional bondage it would have on the present man. We now understand how important it is to handle our mental health. Yes, we need to reach positive emotional health, and this should be encouraged worldwide.

The aggravated connection of emotional health and men should not be disregarded until a crime has been committed, or when there is domestic violence. Men suffering from mental strain is seen all over the news. There's always breaking news of a man or a group of men committing a crime due to their mental state declining. However, what you do not see on the news is men being the victims of domestic violence. Men can certainly be victims of domestic violence. Just the mention of this causes disbelief because men are usually physically superior to women. It seems impossible for a man to be in such a vulnerable situation. But men are susceptible to domestic violence, physical and emotional abuse as well as sexual abuse and assault by intimate partners, family members and predators.

Men experience every kind of abusive event, but their silence causes significant impacts on their mental health and self-value. Along with societies view and opinions, it can be unbearable to live under the stigma that men are to always be strong and stoic. According to society it is impossible for a man to be a victim and if he fails this definition of masculinity he is labeled as weak.

Growing up in a Dark place

How many of us can look back and see all the areas in our past that lead to adult depression? The dark place does not necessarily have to produce an outward reaction, it can also be implosive. Our minds are the resting place of our traumas. This is the main reason our lives have taken the direction it did.

Men we suffer in a number of unseen and unspoken trauma. Childhood traumas like molestation, poverty, abandonment and many more. These deep traumas can stay within us so long that they become part of our personality profile. Creating long lasting triggers and insecurities that as an adult you have long forgotten their origin.

Men with insecurities are viewed as soft and less of a man but it is important to recognize that men also face their own set of insecurities. Society places immense pressure on men to conform to certain ideals of masculinity, such as physical strength, financial success, and emotional stoicism. These expectations can lead to feelings of inadequacy and create breeding grounds for insecurities. Due to these factors, it is crucial that men have access to supportive environments to express their struggles and seek help. These avenues encourage open dialogue, promote mental health awareness and challenge societal stereotypes of masculinity by breaking the silence surrounding men's insecurities. We must normalize conversations about insecurities and foster a culture of acceptance and support.

Men who are susceptible to insecurities have suffered from this burden since their childhood. We must extract the root of our insecurity by acknowledging it and shining a bright light in this dark place. The root of our insecurities can involve societal expectations, body image pressures, career aspirations, emotional expression constraints, relationship insecurities and social comparison. They all can contribute to the problems men struggle with even in their adolescents.

It is essential to address these insecurities and create a supportive environment that allows men to embrace vulnerability, seek help, define masculinity in a healthier and more inclusive way. By acknowledging and addressing man's insecurities, we can promote their overall well-being, better mental health and strive towards a more compassionate society for all men.

Dark places in Phases

As we get older and pass our childhood phrase, we are bombarded with decisions and expectations as young men.

Within this time, behavioral patterns form from a life of dependence to independence. In this time our decisions begin to affect our emotional health. I know of some men who seek ways of escape from their dark beginnings by enlisting in the military.

Young men who decide to go into the military to build skills, travel and learn discipline leave the military completely different then when they arrived. I often recommend that they seek therapy prior to entering, especially if they are displaying depressive symptoms.

I warn them of the absolute possibility of their involvement of war resulting in trauma and PTSD. The mental impact of war and its long-lasting effects become physically, emotionally, and internally clear with these men. These men return home greatly scarred carrying a massive number of triggers and a great need of compassion. Unfortunately, the psychological trauma is overlooked and covered by a flag that only takes notice when covered in blood.

Origins of the dark place within us can begin in so many different areas in our lives. When its origin is in our childhood it will take deeper and more intense therapy. Some of these areas may include the lack of maternal/paternal influence, physical abuse, and/or sexual assault.

Men in their adolescence experience some if not all the characteristics connected to depression due to these factors. Unless a positive element enters their lives to cut off the full impact of depression the onset of this disease will grow within their psyche showing a negative lifestyle and sometimes having a tragic end.

Memories of abusive adolescence can revert a man's mind back to a time of weakness and humiliation. These young men are usually looking for acceptance and belonging but the constant fear of anyone knowing of their struggle causes some to join groups that give a falsehood of acceptance. This acceptance is usually given by others who suffer from the same depressive symptoms and shared backgrounds.

Illusion of Perfection

The pressure to keep a flawless image can take a toll on our mental health, leading to feelings of inadequacy and self-doubt. Many of us have learned the art of hiding our dark places. We have learned how to hide it in a great suit, cover it with cologne, education, polish it and shine it until it no longer looks or feels like what we remember. Some of us are experts in deterring conversation from the subjects that trigger our emotions because of the fear of exposure. The reluctance to share our experiences can perpetuate feelings of isolation, worsen your depression, and hinder your recovery.

Some of us hide our struggle in humor. We have the innate ability to fool everyone around us even people close to us. There are so many unfortunate stories of family members and friends who have lost loved ones to suicide by way of depression. Giving off the illusion of perfection by burying our emotions and putting on brave faces because we live with a constant fear of judgement and stigmatization. It is crucial to understand that men that display the illusion of perfection are not alone in their struggle. We suffer from repressed emotions therefore pushing back our true feelings. Unconsciously suppressing them until we no longer remember the trauma. This can hold for an unlimited amount of time; however, it is not a permanent fix. It is unstable in every way and cannot block a reoccurrence of the trauma from being triggered by anything at any time.

Unveiling the Silence

Conquering the dark place within us must begin with acknowledgement that it exists. Dark places can stem from a traumatic event that has happened to you or around you. However, there is usually one event that happens to men that can become the sole purpose of men carrying unprocessed emotions, sexual assault. This particularly sensitive immensely complex emotional event may create hostility and aggression as a response. Whether it is a memory from childhood, or even adulthood, we turn anger and disappointment upon ourselves. For men this is one of the hardest most significantly challenging events to ever happen to a man's masculinity, yet it's often overlooked and therefore brings on profound psychological implications.

Violent sexual acts upon any gender are difficult to process but regarding men this particular assault its mostly unspoken of and unbelievable in our society. While these acts are often underreported, research suggests that it is more common than previously acknowledged. Traditional gender norms perpetuate the myth that men cannot be victims of sexual assault, or they should be able to defend themselves otherwise. These myths have convinced the world that men are not capable of being vulnerable which would make them inhuman. What is not communicated is how.

Not to be too graphic but sexual assaults can happen anywhere at any time by anyone. No one is exempt from being taken advantage of regardless of their gender, size, or age. Men are of no exception. Predators come in all shapes, sizes, and genders. Usually for adult men the victim is caught off guard. When this occurs men usually experience unprovoked anger alongside depressive symptoms.

The purpose of these attacks whether upon men or women is dominance. However, with men it is a show of dominance and emasculation. Tearing away his pride, self-value, and image both in his personal life and society is the goal. The predators tear away any confidence within their victim. Unfortunately, one of 33 men have experienced an attempt or complete rape in their lifetime.

The probability of it occurring around the ages of 10 and 18 is much higher than adulthood. Nevertheless, this act has nothing to do with his financial status, culture or even age but it has everything to do with power. The odds of a man experiencing victimization in this way increases if their background was impoverished. More than likely, they do not seek therapy or even a medical examination because of the embarrassment of the assault and the physical sensitivity. Young men are experiencing violent acts and traumatic events throughout their communities and within their families. They lack protection and the resources to escape their surroundings.

Society plays a powerful role in the mental challenges of a man. Dictating who should have aid in their emotional health and who should not. Impoverished men and POC with undesirable lives and backgrounds are more likely to be shunned and overlooked.

The opposite holds true for those who do not share these backgrounds, circumstances, and cultures. It also holds true that the scale of emotional wellness between men and women are unbalanced. This creates a challenge for men to get the help they need, and most are too embarrassed to talk about it therefore it gets swept under the rug. The repercussions of men who think their feelings are not valid is low self-esteem and many other depressive symptoms.

Am I Still a Man?

Within the thick walls of our own internal feelings of self, we begin to doubt our own masculinity. This can occur not only with sexual assaults but also with bad decisions and weaknesses that we do not talk about. We are affected by failed relationships and unachieved goals. Failure is a sinkhole which only deepens with each passing day. The world tells the man that he is nothing if he has not succeeded in life, have money, own an expensive car, and have a certain body type. We must always look strong.

The weight upon our backs is always heavy. We are sons, fathers, brothers, uncles etc. Some of us break under the pressure of always carrying the world on our shoulders. Many of us are functioning daily but we are broken. Most of us have given up. This is why this book is so necessary.

It is time for us men to come out of the darkness and heal. We have only covered a small part of why men are suffering in silence. It does not matter how deep and dark your present mental state is there is always a glimmer of hope of healing.

Seek help, despite the many challenges, despite the nagging voice discouraging you from doing it. You were born to carry the mantle of a man. You were built for this fight, and you will win and overcome these obstacles. I am here to tell you that seeking help does not make you less than a man for it takes a man to display courage in his lowest moments. Showing courage in your darkest hour may seem terrifying at first, but once you have passed over the fear of the unknown, you will realize the monster you feared was as big as you imagined. You had the power to overcome it the whole time.

A healed man is an attractive man! He knows his self-worth and he guard his peace. He knows that the hardest part of healing is the first step, accepting that you are suffering from depression. Being honest with yourself is the most powerful tool you can possess. Once you have attained honesty within yourself then you realize step two is achievable, you have the power to stop and destroy the impact it's having on your life. This requires openness to a change in environment, toxic people and being accountable with your own mental health journey. Take the steps to begin therapy so you can process healing in its entirety. Leaving no crumbs, no remnants of it to resurface or attach itself to your personality. Reclaim your sense of self by beginning to rebuild yourself. You are no longer the victim. Healing will turn you into a survivor.

Brothers, you deserve a sounding board. A loud voice stating that your experiences are valid. Your emotional health is as important as anyone else's. Through the initial stages of healing, you will learn that step by step you can navigate through this healing process by staying focused on the bigger picture. You will understand that avoiding your issues will make them impossible to resolve later. You can have more control over your emotions when triggers are dissolved.

Coming out of the darkness is the beginning of self-discovery. It is the releasing of self from the pain that entrapped you. Allow the real you to surface by taking one step at a time toward freedom. I and many other men are here to encourage you to step out of the darkness my friend.

Let's answer that question with our truth. We are ok, we are well and finally, we are good!

Taking the First Step

Embracing Support and Seeking Change

Chapter 2

Get out and Get Help

"From the depths of despair, we find the courage to seek the light, reclaim our lives and rewrite our story."

Depression has the characteristics of quicksand. Sucking you in deeper with every breath. Depleting your life of any light. Applying more pressure until there is no more life left, and you are just a shell of a man. This description of depression was given to me by a young man I knew that was at the end of his rope. He said he felt as if depression had put him in a choke hold of his heartaches and disappointments and he could not stop reliving them.

This young man was in for the fight of his life, but he took the first step by acknowledging and accepting his present state. Depression does not care about your accomplishments it only focuses on your failures. It reminds us that our successes are never good enough. It will punish you daily and strip you of all positivity. Depression causes confusion and unstable thinking. You will struggle and push everyone away yet desperately wants someone to help you. Wanting to express yourself but not able to talk. We are guilty of overthinking and buffering over matters while we tell everyone we are fine with but really, you're not. Depression gifts its host with a constant feeling of emptiness and despair and eventually a death sentence.

This dark entity will not allow happiness to be your dwelling place. Its purpose is to decrease your thirst for life and abandon your future. In this whirlwind of emotions, men search for a safe place but it's usually to no avail. A place where we can express ourselves without criticism and judgement. Some of us are blessed to find this peace but most of us are not.

Most of us will not even look for it. Our minds are always worried about what others will say. In fact, other opinions carry more weight than our own. Our constant fear of being ridiculed and embarrassed will keep our feelings bottled up deep in our subconscious and seen only in our actions when triggered. In this regard, our emotions will not only torture us, but they will begin to torture others.

The darkness of this self-imprisoned place will engulf your life if not exposed and treated. Once it has devoured your most intimate inner circle and it will destroy your outer circle. It will begin to internalize by damaging you physically. It has the characteristics of a parasite that implants its larva in the host of its choice. Like depression, the larvae begin to feed on the organs of the host killing it from the inside. It feeds on the organs and life-giving entities within the body of the host until the larvae are full grown. By then the host is nothing left but a shell of itself. Once the host has been killed it is then the larvae exit. Depression does not voluntarily leave until the soul of its host is no longer there.

When your Freedom is Compromised

The importance of being free of this disease is so great yet most people do not understand its dangers until it's too late. Men suffer from depression 75% more than women. Though this is an incredibly high amount it's not all together hard to imagine. It is because of our inept way of internalizing our emotions causing us to be the prime target for depression. Our men are living day to day with depression having a hopeless mindset while increasing the risk of a shorter life span by 10-12 years because of suicide.

Another example of the urgency to get out and getting help, is when your mind begins to spiral, and your cognitive behavior begins to change. Your mental reasoning and processing begin to slow down causing confusion and brain fog. It will cause problems in your memory and learning capabilities. Beware of these signs and others outlined in this book that will disrupt your healthy outlook.

Let's Start the Process

The best place to start is our opinion of vulnerability. Once we cut the connection of humiliation and emasculation from being vulnerable, we are opening the door to healing. But before we can eliminate it, we must first understand the fear and the origin of it. The fear of vulnerability is taught to men in their childhood. Such as young boys who learn to ride bikes and hurt themselves are usually reprimanded if they show weakness. What normally happens next depends on who is present at that time. When mom is present, she usually nurtures them, brings them in the house and tends to their cuts and bruises. However, if it's a dad that is present the response is quite different. In this case, the correct instruction from dad is of the upmost importance.

The dominant male presence sets the curriculum for male behavior within any community. Dad or any other male figure can dominant a young man's ways and habits including the way he speaks. He will be mimicked by other males in the vicinity. So, if I am taught from an early age not to show any vulnerability, it will be exceedingly difficult to convince me as an adult that it's beneficial to me. This is until the emotional wall constructed between me and my emotions as a child is found and dismantled.

Take this newfound desire to become a better version of yourself by repairing how you think of yourself. Address why you are feeling sad, daily. There are those of us who have mastered the cover up. We keep our sadness private and have our mask on in public. When you find a person who can hide their storm from the rest of the world they are truly in a dangerous place.

I met a young man some time ago by the name of Josh. He was healthy, strong, and very ambitious. He had plans for his future. He gave off the picture of society's man. He was very admired. He always had an entourage of people around him and was highly successful. Watching him move around in his life you would never know there was anything tormenting him privately. Josh has an amazing personality; he was a people magnet. Josh committed suicide after suffering from depression for years. Everyone was in disbelief because of the smile that was always on his face. We learned that he was clinically diagnosed with depression and told no one, not even his family. He was ashamed of his own mental health. He was in control of everything else in his life but could not change this part of himself, so he continued with the façade that everything was great with him. This young man taught me a good lesson. Never take a person by their outward appearance.

Always dig deeper if you care about them because the answers are never on the surface.

Getting Beyond the Mask

We as men have layers and layers that people must unfold to get to really know us. We only allow those that we trust and have proven themselves as trustworthy to get beyond those layers. We must pay attention to ourselves and stop ignoring issues rising within us. No one is more responsible for your mental health than you. Pay attention to your health and be accountable for it. Because we hide behind our falsehood, we are more prone to suppressing our emotions which contributes to our physical breakdown. Go beyond the mask and find out what feelings you are keeping from everyone and why. Ask the tough questions: What is stopping me from opening up and conversing with someone that could help me? Why am I embarrassed by it? Get beyond the mask and face what has kept you a prisoner.

When men experience chronic depression, we may become irritable in our effort to hide our pain. Even in our effort to express our feelings the lack of experience will cause us to unleash our negative emotions upon anyone. With my own personal experience with depression, I became difficult to be around because I could not figure out my life. I began experiencing insomnia. My mind was buffering and would not allow me to rest. If you find yourself in this state, you must get out and seek help.

Some of us begin to seek distraction from things that worry us. Taking more risks where normally we wouldn't do such things. We become reckless, doing things that are not within our character. They used to call it a midlife crisis, but actually it's the onset of depression because we are getting older, and our life is changing. Accepting the fact that we are not as young as we used to be and not as physically fit. It can take a toll on a man's mentality. So, we begin to behave in ways to keep our youth intact instead of embracing a new journey in our lives.

While depression can feel overwhelming remind yourself that you can recover from it. Regardless of how big our thoughts are making the events that are stagnating us, we can overcome them. It is a challenge for us to seek help. It is a challenge for us to accept help too because we have been trained by society that we are weak by doing so and will be judged harshly. It makes you wonder of the struggle men are involved in mentally. They want to converse with someone but are afraid to because of the constant pressure of displaying the manly image. This is a man's daily emotional tug of war.

Do not Wait too Late

Suicide finalizes everything. It diminishes your hopes and dreams. It will rob you of making amends with someone you care about. Harming yourself can be the most heart wrenching thing you can do to those who love you. It gives them emptiness and confusion because there is no justice to seek. There are no questions answered, just a void where there was once your loved one. Why inflict your loved ones in this way? Why die in shame and guilt when you can live in forgiveness and a new beginning? Learn the benefits of having a community of men who have all made mistakes. Listen to other men tell their stories and realize you are not alone.

Educate yourself about this condition and learn the seriousness of it and why it should not be taken lightly.

Find out about the treatments, therapies, support groups, private therapy, etc. Reinforce the fact that seeking help is a sign of strength and courage. It will prove to your family that you understand the value you are to them. They will see your emotional struggle is not stronger than their need and love for you.

Resolve the issues connected to depression, do not sacrifice your body, time, money, health, and relationships for it. Unlearn the taught behavior towards therapy. This damaging societal theory is the reason there are so many men in their graves too early, dying full of promise. They are not fulfilling their destiny nor impacting the world with their gifts.

I am a firm believer that our lives are for others. We are of service to each other. Your life has meaning why not go as far as you can leaning everything you can about yourself.

Making the Best decision for Myself

After deciding to get out of depression, be patient with yourself. Understand and learn what to expect on this journey to emotional health. Do not rush the process by jumping ahead. Each step is there for a reason. The goal is to be rid of the emotional turmoil and any addictions that may have latched on to you. To function without horrible thoughts, traumatic events replaying in your mind and yielding to an escape mechanism that drives you deeper into that hole.

Trust yourself to get through this. Be open and honest about your feelings and concerns. If you are dealing with trust issues or low self-esteem, this can prove to be difficult to do. Trust issues can make it challenging for individuals with depression to form and keep healthy relationships. They may struggle to confide in others fearing judgment, betrayal, or abandonment. This can lead to feelings of isolation and even more depressive symptoms. Trust issues can make it difficult for individuals to seek help and support as they may have doubts about the intentions and reliability of others.

Low self-esteem is often intertwined with depression, negative self-perception, feelings of worthlessness, and self-criticism which can contribute to persistent depressive symptoms. Men with low self-esteem may struggle with feelings of inadequacy, self-doubt, and distorted views of their own abilities. They have a negative self-image. This can further fuel depressive thoughts and emotions.

Both trust issues and low self-esteem can create a negative cycle in depression, especially in men. They can reinforce each other making it difficult for individuals to break free from depressive symptoms. So, it is important for men experiencing depression to address these underlying issues and seek professional help to develop healthier coping strategies and improve their overall well-being. Being honest with oneself is an essential part of addressing and managing depression.

 Listen to me guys, for us to be honest with ourselves, we must acknowledge and accept our emotions, thoughts and experiences without judgment or denial. This self-awareness will allow us to recognize and understand our depressed symptoms, triggers, and our patterns. It will enable us to gain insight into the underlying causes of our depression. Most unresolved trauma and negative thought patterns are simply unmet needs.

Make an appointment to be treated by a doctor so they may diagnose the problem. A good therapist or support group will actively listen to you and not interrupt you. They will empathize and form an alliance with you. For men, the sense of belonging goes a long way.

Hearing other men discuss their issues freely can automatically lift a load from the shoulders of the listeners. Taking notice of not only what is said but the fact that others are going through shared experiences like you. Seeing men react to problems that you also have will create a mindfulness of self.

Take note that the deeper the issues are the more uncomfortable you may become when getting closer to them. This is normal. This is healing. It is like having a cut on your finger. You do not feel the pain in the beginning. You feel it when it begins to heal. It becomes sore and sensitive to the touch. But this is part of the process. Without a little discomfort we are just walking open wounds.

Suppression often involves distorted thinking patterns and negative self-beliefs. So being honest with yourself will help you recognize these negative beliefs and challenge their validity. By questioning and reframing negative thoughts, men can develop a more realistic and compassionate perspective towards themselves. This process of self-reflection and self-evaluation can gradually replace self-critical thoughts with more positive and empowering ones.

Transparency

My moment of getting out and getting help came when I realized that depression was quietly controlling my life. When I saw how my behavior had changed toward people that I loved. I stopped caring about myself and I went from a fit lifestyle and working out several times a week to gaining terrible weight. I could barely climb the stairs. I ate nothing but comfort food and stopped caring about my appearance. I went from wearing suits and hats to sweatpants and t shirts. Depression affected my relationships. I did not care about myself so therefore I treated others the same way. Yes guys, men who suffer from depression show it in their relationships. It's not spoken of but men who are in the state of depression attract women and partners who emasculate them. Their role in the relationship becomes blurred and so does their self-respect.

If you doubt this theory, step back and listen to how the people close to you talk about you, to you and around you. Look at how they treat you. You will soon realize that people treat you the way you allow them to and the way you treat yourself.

Be honest with yourself with the presence and impact depression is having in your life. This could motivate us men to seek professional help and support. This will also involve acknowledging the need for assistance and recognizing that reaching out for help is a sign of strength not weakness. Appraisal can lean us men to engage in therapy, counseling, or other forms of support to develop coping strategies, learning new skills, and receiving guidance in managing their depression.

I got out and I got help. I took the fragments of my life and began to put the pieces back together. It took time to unlearn living in emotional pain. It took more time to stop grieving my parents' sudden deaths and a divorce which all happened within the same year. It took time to recover and forgive myself for straining the relationship between myself and my children. I had to stop blaming myself for everything that went wrong and accept that I was on this path for a reason. Only when I ceased feeling sorry for myself did I gain the strength needed to allow others to be accountable for their own actions in every scenario in my life. I freed myself through forgiveness.

Honestly, by having a clear understanding of the need of my personal growth it enabled me to identify and adopt healthy coping strategies that worked for me. They included engaging in self-care activities like practicing relaxation techniques, setting realistic goals, establishing a supportive network, and seeking professional treatment. By being honest with myself concerning what worked for me and what did not work for me, I was able to create an effective toolkit to manage my depression.

I forgave myself and others and sought after the help I needed to become the man I was destined to be. I released the pent-up emotions that were driving me deeper into depression. I got the support needed and deserved. Guys do not go another day without relieving yourself of burdens too heavy for you to carry. Be free of it and live your life with purpose.

Navigating the Storm

Understanding and Managing Life's Pressures

Chapter 3

The Stress of It All

"Men are forged in the fires of stress, emerging stronger and more resilient."

Let's face it, life is full of stress. This is unavoidable. The best advice for stress is to fine tune our adaptability towards it. Understanding that stress and depression run hand in hand. Overbearing situations with unfolded solutions can cause any man to spiral. Men are required to have the answer. But what causes us to spiral when we cannot find the answers? Let's dig deeper.

What's bugging you?

What stresses us? What storms are we bearing? Is your storm changing your behavior? Stress is a high state of mental tension we feel when confronted with a demanding situation. It is also when a situation negatively changes, or something changes that exceeds our ability to cope. It all comes down to our perception of it. However, how we perceive an event differs man to man. Men often prefer a solution-oriented approach to stress management. We focus on finding the root causes of our stress and actively seeking practical solutions to address them. This may include creating to do lists, making action plans, or seeking advice from our trusted friends. Some men find silence and spending time alone perfect for recharging and processing our thoughts and emotions.

Take time for calming activities such as reading, meditation, listening to music or engaging in hobbies. This can provide a sense of relaxation and help reduce stress levels. While men may tend to handle stress individually, seeking support from others can beneficial.

Men have the tendency to experience depression at any stage of their lives but the normal peak age for depression is around 40 and after. However, this can occur whenever a man faces approaching drastic changes within their lives. Talking to trusted friends, family members or even a therapist can provide an outlet for expressing emotions, gaining perspective, and receiving guidance. However, with men usually a physical activity helps us relieve our stress. Engaging in physical exercise, such as going to the gym, running, playing sports, or even practicing martial arts can be an effective way for men to release pent up stress and tension. Exercise promotes the release of endorphins which are natural mood boosters and stress reducers.

Some of us men can handle stress a lot better than others, but it all depends on our coping abilities. How we handle them also depends on the circumstances or the problem. Stress can either be short term or long term. Only when stress goes beyond our coping abilities is when stress becomes a problem. Accumulating stress can be a major problem. When there is a constant stream of changes to our routine stress will appear along with frustration. Once this begins to happen, the weight of our stress will leave your mind and body in chaos. Years of internalizing our feelings will eventually show. Verbalizing our stress may come out with aggression inadvertently pushing people away that mean to help.

The accumulation of unexpressed stress can become too heavy to carry, and at some point, change our quality of life. The lack of the proper tools to handle stress causes men to have a higher diagnosis of chronic depression where the symptoms can be evident in their physical health. We are more prone to strokes, heart attacks, decreased immune function, alcohol use, drug abuse and domestic violence.

Another way men show stress is by showing anger, frustration and displaying uncontrollable mood swings. Our behavior changes dramatically. We will stop engaging with our loved ones and begin to isolate ourselves in fear of our vulnerable state becoming exposed. I have met many men who because of their lack of communication have problems within their homes with their families. Where they show their displeasure oppose verbalizing it because this leads to miscommunication and sometimes violence.

It is crucial that we explore the causes of stress in men, how it affects us and how we can manage it better. One of the major sources of stress for every man is social expectation of us being the breadwinner and the provider of our families. There is extreme pressure that is on us daily to make sure that our families have everything they need and then some. Though you can find in any home both partners working and sharing expenses society remains in the mindset that the man is solely responsible and should be holding the bulk of the responsibility. We all want to be perfect providers but there are times we fall short. I can speak for myself, it's major for me to be able to support my family anything less than the best upsets me. Not having our bills paid and the ability to enjoy extracurricular activities will immediately make me stressed.

I know the feeling of financial struggle, and this is something we as men will work countless hours to prevent.

So instead of killing ourselves men let us learn money management and investing for our peace of mind.

Leadership has been handed to the man since the beginning of time and the quality of our leadership places a vital role within our family. Understanding the balancing act of work fulfillment, family responsibilities and self-care is something that should be taught early in life. But when it is not, the man grows into uncertainty of the roles allotted to him. Men need encouragement that they can be successful even in a financially unstable world because they hold the proper tools and the proper training, even if it is self-taught.

We must cut off any areas in our lives that could lead to unbearable stress. I have arrived at my home needing to unload my day and find a quiet place to relax but my family and other matters require my attention. We have all been there, but priority comes first, which usually puts your mental health at the back of the line. Though we try to answer all the calls connected to our roles as men we can never get to them all which leaves us feeling incomplete and inconsistent. Nevertheless, no one can pour from an empty cup, so take time to recharge so that you can give what matters to you the best version of yourself.

Amongst many other personal stressors there are the environmental and societal ones. You may wonder how this may affect our mental health, but it certainly does. Our country is experiencing an increasing amount of gun violence which can make anyone feel unsafe. Men, we have an instinct to protect ourselves and our family. Keeping our family safe is essential to our well-being.

There are men all over this country living with the aftermath of violence in their homes and communities.

Unsettled minds normally make rash decisions like purchasing weapons with the sole purpose of protecting but not having a well thought out plan or having any training for safety. So, with the violative atmosphere in our country educate yourself on gun safety within the home. Educate your children on gun safety and precautions in reference to school shootings.

Living in poverty whether for a fleeting period or long term can both be stressful for a man. Any length of time within this stressful world can cause emotional strain and begin generational cycles if not rectified. Men living in the world of poverty are usually living in depression. They are brow beaten by society, living with the constant feeling of inferiority and defeat.

These men are recognized everywhere throughout our cities and suburbs committing crimes, homelessness and sleeping on the street, in prison or dead because of their background and the lack of concern from our society. Most are living in pure desperation. Many suffering from mental illness and emotional dysfunction are overlooked and discriminated against in the judicial system therefore adding to their already stressful life.

The consequences on chronic untreated mental illness for men is significant. We must monitor ourselves more. Pay attention to how our bodies are responding to controlled stressors and uncontrolled stressors. If you notice that you are experiencing constant headaches, digestive problems, cardiovascular problems or even anxiety, seek medical attention. It may be related to stress. Major health conditions usually start small so do not ignore them because at this point the treatment may be less evasive. These minor symptoms should be recognized early but if ignored can become incurable.

To have a successful journey towards living without depression learn to avoid unhealthy coping mechanisms. Prioritize self-care and beware of your stress levels. Your self care must have tools that are ready for when you need them. Schedule alone time for your peace of mind. Have a conversation with your family about your mental health. Join a support group or take the initiative to start one. Do your research and find a group of men that are like minded. This is vital to your development so that you feel safe and can be transparent with your issues.

What's in your tool belt?

Every man has their own way of relaxing and recharging. Mine is meditation in a dark room. This is my way of turning off the world and removing myself from everything that stressed me. My wife and I respect each other's differences. We also respect the fact that we each need space for a long day. It is our way of caring for each other's mental health. After we talk a little or a lot depending on our day, we have dinner and then we go in separate rooms, temporarily. She usually continues her work in her office, and I go to my prayer room to meditate. It helps that our children are adults so we can organize our time in ways that help us only.

For those of us that are single and living that single life having fun is usually top priority, but it also comes with its low points too. The number of men that are single are between the ages of 25 and 54 have increased dramatically. The dating scene is a lot more difficult than it used to be. Some of the new generations really do not care about being married or being too attached to anyone. They opt for financial security rather than settling down. However, studies show that being single for too long can result in anxiety and depression due to isolation. Being single may give you the time and opportunity to explore and live life on your own terms but it can also invite fear of future relationships. Men experience anxiety due to lack of confidence because of prior relationships and the possibility of failing again.

Though we all stress our battle is to not allow it to become chronic and overwhelm us. But if it does you can overcome it if the symptoms are noticed early. If stress is something that you deal with, exercise some self-care, and put the proper tools in place. Start by acknowledging that stress is affecting your life on a higher level. Get a checkup guys, your way of life may depend on it. Life is stressful enough without adding a medical ailment to it.

Prevent the need for medications, hospitals or worse for your family to endure. Creating medical bills and straining your finances because of something that is preventable is just not worth it.

Get together with your boys, family or even a professional and talk. Find a safe environment and even if you do not take part in the beginning just listening to other men express themselves could help you know that you are not alone. If these options are not available, book a hotel room for the weekend with nothing on the agenda but relaxation. Schedule a massage for yourself or get together with friends and attend a game to let off some steam.

The overall message here is to not allow the stress to deplete you and the life you have built for yourself or the life you are building. Understanding the effects of stress and becoming more educated about its damaging effects on the mind and body will help you navigate your way to a more self-care routine. At the end of the day the goal is to have a less stressful and fulfilling life.

Reframing the Narrative

Transforming Setbacks into Opportunities

Chapter 4

Removing A Failure Mindset

"Failure should be our teacher, not our undertaker.

It's a delay, not our defeat. It's a temporary detour, not a dead-end-street." William Ward

Whatever power that exists over you was given power by you. Willing your mind to failure will indeed make you a failure. But how and when did failure become an obstacle instead of an opportunity? To overcome an obstacle, it is important to first understand it as well as the core of it.

The power of failure can be excruciating for some, traumatizing, and debilitating for others. For some men, it has always been an accepted part of their life. Failure can feel like a 3-ton anvil tied around your neck wearing you down and stumbling any progress. Depending on your frame of mind, failure can either be expected, accepted or both. Let's get deeper into this.

Definition of A Failure Mindset

Failure is defined as perceiving the lack of achievement or your desired outcome or goal. It can be a heavy feeling of disappointment and frustration about yourself. A feeling that generates sadness and possible depression if your efforts do not lead to your desired results. Depression that can create a failure mindset is often connected with major depressive disorder (MDD). Major depressive disorder is a mental health condition characterized by persistent feelings of sadness, hopelessness, and a lack of interest or pleasure in activities. It can affect your ability to think clearly, make decisions or maintain positive motivation.

Most men take failure as a personal and direct impression of themselves. Their worth and number of accomplishments are tied to society's impression of them.

They measure their success by the amount and weight of their failures. We as men are normally extremely hard on ourselves, intentionally. When a man experiences depression, we develop a negative and distorted belief of ourselves and our abilities. This negative self-perception can lead to a failure mindset, where we tend to believe we are incapable of succeeding or achieving our goals. We may view setbacks or challenges as confirmation of our perceived inadequacy, leading to a cycle of self-doubt, low-esteem, and diminished confidence.

Some of us were introduced to failure early in life. As children we remember the lessons that we were failures and that our accomplishments would be minuscule. There are some of us that are labeled as a failure because we favor someone else's physical appearance. Young men who resemble their fathers are usually looked upon as replicas of them, especially if the father betrayed the mother.

The life of this man child is full of accusations, low expectations and trauma that usually put the child on a path that will justify the prediction of them. This proves how a failure mindset can begin in a man's childhood and have a lasting effect on them throughout their lives. Let's cover a failure mindset combined with depression.

Symptoms of Depression

The failure mindset associated with depression can be a result of a range of factors including:

Negative self-talk: Men dealing with depression often engage in self-critical and self-depreciating thoughts, reinforcing a belief that they are failures or unworthy of success.

Cognitive Distortion: Depression can distort a man's thinking patterns leading to cognitive warping such as all-or-nothing thinking, over generalization, over thinking and over personalization. These deformities contribute to a skewed perception of failure and a dismissed ability to see one's achievements and strengths.

Lack of Motivation: Depression can sap a man's energy and motivation. It can become difficult to set or pursue life goals. The lack of motivation can further reinforce the belief that success is unattainable.

Feeling of hopelessness: Depression often brings on a sense of hopelessness. It challenges men to see a way out of their perceived failures. This feeling of hopelessness can further perpetuate the failure mindset.

Many of us know of someone who was molded from childhood to failure. They go throughout their lives with the mindset that nothing will work out for them. These young men grow to have an inner hate for themselves and the world.

They harbor a resentment towards those who are successful, even though they receive the same opportunities. The opportunities are available but usually their chances are much harder to reach success for several reasons that involve economic, cultural, and societal barriers.

It also resonates with our possible negative stereotypes, core belief systems, expectations, and values.

Unfortunately, these are usually structured early in our lives.

I have met many young men who have struggled since childhood with a failure mindset. Believing that their destiny is to fail, and that success is completely out of reach. As a man who was raised in the city, I see these types of men every day. So, I made a mission to help as many men as possible to change their mindset regarding themselves. During many of my counseling sessions I hear stories of trauma and the impact the little boy inside is still enduring. You can still hear the screaming for help and guidance from them even in their adulthood.

Many still struggle with comparing themselves to others and feeling defeated. These young men know what it is to feel unwanted and unappreciated by people who say they love them and from society in general. The unfortunate part of all of this is that there is always someone lingering around these very impressionable young men waiting like vultures to capture them in their developing years. These men are fed toxic ideas about the world and given false brotherhood with many strings attached.

They normally live in the same community as them and possibly have the same upbringing. In economically challenged areas as well as affluent and wealthy environments these persons exist who have addictive yet negative persuasive rhetoric which attracts young men at the most vulnerable stages.

Procuring a failure mindset that originates from the community you grew up in does not depend on a particular zip code or tax bracket. It is universally omnipresent.

Fine Tuning your Mind

Some escape this misfortune by somehow having the ability to stay focused on creating a better life for themselves. There is an off chance that the power that pushes their success is fear. Fear of returning to the past. Nevertheless, those who are entangled in the web of failure find it impossible to be free. Some do not make it out at all. But for those who are still struggling with failure you must conquer this before it destroys your future.

Failure has a way of causing you to self-sabotage everything that you touch. It causes you to doubt your abilities and second guess all your decisions. I met a young man who was an incredible artist. But because he lived with a failure mindset his entire life the fear stopped him from advancing. He would paint a few pieces and as soon as someone criticized his work he would not paint again for months. His lack of confidence caused him to miss opportunities and stagnated his professional growth.

His failure mindset began to affect his career. He would hesitate to take on new projects or put his work in galleries. He was convinced that he would not succeed. It not only affected him professionally, but it affected his private life as well. He lost the ability to maintain a meaningful relationship with someone. He started pushing people away, rejecting people and believing that he did not deserve to be loved. The loneliness within his personal life further fueled his negative mindset of himself and he saw that not having someone in his life made him unworthy of love.

How do you help change the mind of someone who has learned throughout their entire life that failure is normal?

How do you convince a person to have faith in themselves and trust people again? We had many discussions between myself and this gentleman I have concerning this subject. Most, if not, all find it incredibly hard to unlearn this mindset. The artist after some time began to meet people who loved his work and encouraged him to continue. He began to understand whose opinion of his mattered most, his own. He soon began to compartmentalize criticism as positive and gave himself a chance to grow by perfecting his work. Though this was a difficult experience for him he gained a tool that would help him emotionally throughout his life.

He soon realized that having a failure mindset was holding him back and stopping him from living and fulfilling his dreams. This young man now understands the power of his mind. Understanding the importance of having the right people around him was essential for his journey. So, he surrounded himself with supportive and encouraging people who believed in his potential. The changing of his mindset attracted the right people in his life and changed his personal life. He stopped being so hard on himself and understood that his setbacks are just opportunities for growth. To remove a failure mindset, it helps to learn your triggers.

Learn what makes you feel inadequate and self-conscious. What makes you doubt yourself? Conquer the fear of rejection and judgement. Increase your confidence and stay motivated. Put emphasis on growing a healthy mindset when it comes to failure. People normally attribute their failures to lack of ability or effort. They also connect them to luck or circumstance. The way failure can be received whether internally or externally can create resiliency and give the ability to bounce back. It will also determine the struggle and possible prolonged negative emotions. We know that experiencing failure can undermine your self-efficiency. This can destroy a man's self-confidence and his motivation. Develop a healthy self-esteem that is not solely dependent on external successes. This is major to controlling the negative effects of failure.

The Influential Power of Money

Managing money is an area amongst us men that brings out strong emotions. We become frustrated and angry with ourselves for not being able to effectively manage our money. Our financial difficulties create feelings of failure. We began to feel ashamed and embarrassed if our money management skills affect our family negatively.

We experience thoughts of being less of a man if we cannot upkeep a standard of living that others expect of us. Societal expectations of being financially responsible and successful fall heavily upon our shoulders. Anything less than being capable is a failure to us. This can have a negative impact on our self-esteem and sense of identity as a man.

This is usually a tricky topic for us men if we are struggling to be more balanced balance in our lives. We normally avoid the topic if we can find the quickest way out of the conversation of money. During our avoidance we may ignore bills, avoid discussing finances or even engage in impulsive spending habits to temporarily escape the reality of our financial situation. However, if we look at our struggle with money from a different angle, we will see it as a wake-up call for us to seek knowledge, gain resources and support. That will improve our financial literacy and skills. You must be motivated to learn about budgeting, saving, and investing to regain control of your finances. If necessary, reach out to financial advisors and counselors or even support groups so that you will have the guidance you need to help in managing your finances. Recognize the need for help and actively seek support. This is a positive step towards addressing financial challenges.

Managing our money properly continues to be something that we struggle with one point or the other and this can affect a man greatly. We often associate our self-worth and identity with success, our achievements and how productive we are through money.

Discover the link between money and your mental health. Educate yourself and allow knowledge to offer healthier opportunities.

The Rabbit Hole

When we experience failure it's nearly impossible not to display disappointment and therefore destroy our productivity. Laziness for men often creates a rabbit hole in which everything in our lives is affected. Triggers that involve money can leave a man spiraling. This is true in my case. I remember when my wife and I were recently married. I noticed shortly after our wedding that I did not stay on track with our finances. The fear of disappointing her and falling behind on our bills was enormous. I researched ways to have a stronger grasp on my finances. I also learned investing and was able to help others. I pretended many times to be in control of everything so not appearing less of a man. After panicking for a while I changed my response to this. I chose to stop calling it a failure and saw it more as a leaning curb and I promised myself that I would never allow it to happen again by staying aware, becoming educated, and never crossing my bottom line, no matter what.

Importance of The Correct Response

Prolonged failure in a man's life can manifest fear of failure. Fear creates a psychological barrier that will hinder men from taking risks or pursuing their goals. Just like the artist we spoke about earlier; failure will have you expecting negative consequences such as embarrassing criticism and a loss of status. Failure can produce avoidance behaviors and being reluctant to step out of your comfort zone. Failure is in the mind of the man. Therefore, the tendency to compare ourselves to others who appear more successful or productive will magnify our feelings of failure and inadequacy. Social expectations and stigma surrounding masculinity can contribute to feelings of shame because men often perceive laziness as a sign of weakness and lack of masculinity.

Changing your perspective on failure requires changing your mindset on your abilities. Change your ability by showing more effort in the areas in your life that are challenging and develop a healthier attitude towards the twists and turns in your journey. Put more emphasis on learning from your mistakes and push past challenges by looking for opportunities to improve yourself. Be aware of perfectionism. Take caution not to set extremely lofty standards for yourself for this can create a high fear of failure. This can rob you of living a full life. Because living life in fear is a life in bondage. Work on producing a healthy mental state when it comes to failure. Embrace your struggle and set realistic goals for yourself and navigate through your shortcomings. Success comes from trial and error.

Step over Life's Potholes

There is a psychological terminology called learnt helplessness. This is when a person feels powerless to change their circumstances. This behavior causes you to feel as if you cannot change the direction of their life. I am here to tell you this is false. This behavior develops when a man has repeated failures and disappointments in their lives. We unknowingly begin to associate our decisions with future fail. In this regard, a man should decide to take the steps to change his mindset, but they usually convince themselves that it will never work out and therefore form a defeated consciousness. This will cause the assigning of failure to their personality and their character which will affect every decision they make throughout their adulthood.

 Men in this headspace become passive resigned. They stop trying to achieve and settle for mediocrity. They must challenge their negative impulses and emotions when it involves their goals. Create a form of resiliency when it involves failure. Learn to bounce back from failures and learn to solve problems instead of reacting in a negative emotional way. Do not socially compare yourself to anyone else because we all have our own journey to healthy mental well-being.

When positive psychological changes have occurred whether from trauma or adversity, new perspectives, and deeper understanding of yourself will create better perspectives of self, greater resilience, and new transformations in your life.

Man to man, do not beat yourself up guys. It is natural to feel disappointed in yourself sometimes. It is natural to feel as if you have disappointed everyone in your life, but no one is perfect. There is no one on this planet that gets it right every time. Do not give up on yourself and learn from your mistakes.

"Success is not final: failure is not fatal: It is the courage to continue that counts." Winston Churchill

Recognizing Weak Links

Strengthening the Bonds of Resilience

Chapter 5

When there's a Chink in my Armor

"Strength lies not in the absence of vulnerabilities, but in the courage to embrace them and grow stronger."

Is it just me or do you all picture a Superman S on your chest sometimes like I do? Sometimes I feel invincible. In my fantasy my armor is spotless and shining like a diamond making me feel like I am unstoppable and powerful. That is until life reminds me that I am a scared and at times a vulnerable human being. At this point I snap out of it and realize I am too old for fairy tales and must live in this world along with everyone else. Guys we have these moments and there is nothing wrong with them, but we must accept the days that we do not feel as powerful.

Your Slip is Showing

Your slip is showing is an old African American saying that was directed toward young women who were wearing a thin skirt or dress with no lining therefore needing an undergarment called a slip which covered her privacy. If the slip were too long or not worn appropriately and if seen by an older woman in the community, they would be scolded that their slip was showing. This was their way of saying that you were exposed and her upbringing questioned. This old saying made me think of how men are viewed in our society. A mere slip up and we are exposed and considered weak. But in this case an under garment cannot fix the problem. It becomes a permanent label for us.

One thing we all have in common as men, we hate to be thought of as weak. This is a no no both in public and in private. However, when it is discovered, it can cause a whirlwind of emotional and unexpectant behavior by us.

But this isn't true for all of us men? We do not all respond the same way. There are those of us that can handle embarrassing moments with a lot more grace than others. It all depends on our perspective and tolerance.

As a newly married man the last thing I want my wife to think of me is weak. But the transparency of marriage makes that utterly impossible to avoid. However, the more I think about relationships the more I realize that vulnerability is something that should be seen and accepted. Your spouse should see you vulnerable. We are all human beings who experience a spectrum of emotions and feelings. Emotions and feelings are temporary spaces that should be thought of as such. Once completely accepted, even in a non-flattering light, it is a healthy way of viewing each other which offers forgiveness towards each other.

Though this is the best way to view vulnerability towards men the reality is quite different. So, how do we handle things when we discover a chink in our armor? When is your weakness exposed for all to see?

Deny, deny, and deny!

The first thing we do as men when a weakness is present is deny it. Disregarding our problems is something we all use as a response to a subject we are not ready to talk about. We become defensive when the topic of vulnerability is revealed. This reaction stems from a desire to protect our self-image at all costs. We downplay or even dismiss our frailties as a defense mechanism. Some of us choose to resist facing them because we are uncertain of how we will react to them. The look of embarrassment when you do not have control for a man is detrimental. Society reminds us of how we must handle everything in our lives and that is with strength. We are only strong, independent, and self-reliant in all situations. Unfortunately, this is not reality. So, during this tug of war between society and reality frustration builds within us and we opt out. We shut down and become mute especially when pressured.

Some of us experience frustration to the level of anger. We become frustrated with ourselves for not meeting our own expectations or societal ideas of strength. This emotional response can also arise from fear of judgement, or a sense of shame associated with having this weakness. These incredibly strong feelings in a man are usually clear in his behavior which can quickly become violative.

The Surfacing of our Emotions

Most crimes towards women are committed by men and unfortunately, most of these men are dealing with some sort of depression. Their mental state usually stems from unhealed childhood traumas. The history of these men always involves them being assaulted in the most vulnerable state. Predators are born from this. Their trauma lingers on to their adulthood and it is unleashed upon anyone who triggers these emotions. This brings on the topic of violence towards women. A concerning number of attacks have been happening in the past few years against women by men who are under tremendous emotional and mental duress.

Rejection has always been part of a man's life. All fathers have had that particular talk with their boys about how to handle rejection from women and from the world. Unfortunately, it's just part of being a man but when these lessons are not instructed properly a young man will begin to internalize these minor rejections as a personal attack against him. Regardless of our feelings towards rejection there is absolutely no excuse for any man to ever hit or be violent towards a woman. However, the ones who target women are usually those who are dealing with issues from their past or their present in which they reveal that the chink in their armor revolves around negative emotions involving women. His trauma has now turned into regression.

 emotions. If men are prone to violence or have experienced hostile environments along their youth it will be considered normal behavior for them. More than likely, they will show this same behavior in their adulthood. I have personally never seen so many attacks against women until recent. It has become so that more and more women are afraid to be alone whether inside or outside. Why are so many men attacking women? What is the source of our anger? This must be addressed.

Many of us men live with unmanaged anger. Depression can sometimes manifest itself as irritability, frustration, and anger. Men living with depression do not have healthy coping mechanisms nor do they seek proper support for their anger. Therefore, it can manifest itself in harmful and violent attacks towards others. This includes attacks against women who are in relationship with these unhealed men.

Most women are unaware of the storm that lies beneath his smile or docile demeanor until it is too late.

Some of us who are living with depression turn to self-medicating. We begin to look for ways to disengage with our inner storm. We use substances to impair our judgement, lower inhibitions and increase the likelihood of engaging in violent behavior. The impact of depression leads to feelings of isolation and withdrawal from societal interactions. Individuals with depression feel disconnected from others. Their often-exaggerated feelings of frustration and anger inadvertently cause them to isolate themselves. This isolation can also limit access to social support networks that could help mitigate violent tendencies.

It is important to also acknowledge that societal norms, cultural influences and learned behaviors from our environments play a role in how men express themselves. There are signs of other conditions that may begin to surface like personality disorders, anger management or impulsive control disorders. These conditions can further increase the chances of violent behavior if left untreated and unaddressed.

My Approval of Me

Let's address the struggle we have when it comes to acceptance. Why is it important for us to feel accepted by society? Why do we feel defeated when a woman does not accept us? I went to the gym the other day to work out and people watch. It is something I do sometimes. I took a break from the set I was working on and decided to scan my environment. I decided to specifically look at the men and their behavior. Just from my observations there were 3 categories of men present. There were those that were there to work out and focus on their health like I was, but this was only about 4 or 5 including myself. Then there was "That guy." Those who come to the gym to show off their bodies and low key intimidate others. We all know them. They usually wear the tightest fit they can find and watch whoever is watching them. There are predators. These guys are looking for any female or male who gives them eye contact. They are usually following some unsuspecting lady around acting as if they know everything about the gym other than how to get to one. But then I noticed the 3rd man. These guys are looking to improve themselves only for acceptance. They normally are the ones observing others to see what machines they should use so they can look like everyone else. These insecure men idolize "that guy," thinking that this will make their lives so much better.

Nevertheless, it really does not matter what group you fall into; acceptance is the goal. The real work starts on the inside however, the mind can be the most underworked muscle in a man's entire body.

This is not just a man thing everyone suffers from wanting acceptance on some part of the scale, what matters is how you allow it to affect you. However, us men searching for acceptance can lead us down the wrong road. The desperate need for acceptance has caused some of our young men to follow the wrong crowd, commit crimes and become a nuisance within their community. There are socioeconomic factors within their decisions to be in these groups which are usually exceedingly difficult to get out of and are very manipulative. If you took a deeper look into the lives of these men, you would notice similar backgrounds, most have lived in the same disadvantaged community, they come from the same family structure and the leader is usually an older man portraying the dysfunctional father figure.

Men who gravitate to this usually lack early support from their families and/or community who see this type of behavior amongst their men as normal and in some cases, their behavior is encouraged. Positive role models are far and few between in these communities and are usually thought of as weak and insignificant within their circles.

Abandonment is another universal human experience that can affect individuals of any gender. There is no specific gender or sex that is affected greater but amongst men its reach is much deeper and usually not seen. The feeling of abandonment or rejection by someone significant, whether it be a partner, family member, friend or even a social group can leave an emptiness that can last a lifetime. This can be the result of many things like the end of a relationship, loss of a loved one or even the sense of being alone and disconnected from others. Men experience abandonment in different ways and for distinct reasons. Let's discuss some of the common causes of abandonment that affect men.

Relationship breakdowns: Romantic relationships ending can cause a man to feel abandoned by their partners especially if the breakup was considered unexpected or they were deeply invested in the relationship. Parent abandonment. Many do not believe that men suffer from the abandonment of their parents, but this can affect us greatly. We just suffer in silence. We feel the emotional unavailability if the first woman in our life was not there, or our first role model is not present. This can have long lasting effects on us and carry on into our adult relationships.

Abandonment at an early age can affect our self-worth and ability to understand the importance of our roles within a relationship or family structure. It is unfortunate how the same scenario can play out in your adult years that traumatized you in your childhood. We understand how difficult growing up in a single parent home can be yet there are men that have inflicted this same pain upon their own children.

Friendship loss. There are those that may not feel as if losing a friend is important but certain friendships like childhood friendships or people who have entered your life at a pivotal moment are one of the most painful experiences one can endure. Friendships are an important source of support and connection for a man. These relations are an essential need in every man's life.

Career or financial setbacks. Men may feel triggers of abandonment if setbacks in their careers occur causing them to lose their opportunities for growth. The feeling of rejection from a professional standpoint when the chance to advance has been taken from you. This can cause regression to form in your life. It can also create negative self-value and belief that no one sees the value in you.

It is important to recognize that everyone's experience of abandonment is unique, and the impact can vary from person to person. It is also important to seek support and understanding when experiencing feelings of abandonment.

Talk to a trusted friend, family member or even a mental health professional that can help you process these emotions and develop coping strategies to navigate through them. Remember, seeking support is a sign of strength, and there are resources available to help us men cope with and overcome feelings of abandonment.

How do I Cope?

The absence of a nurturing relationship and emotional support can contribute to feelings of isolation and exacerbate the risk of developing depression. In certain communities' young men can find themselves bandaging their feelings in alcohol and using this coping mechanism to numb emotional pain or mask underlying mental health issues like depression.

Substance abuse can further exaggerate depressive symptoms and create a cycle of self-destructive behavior. These men create barriers so not to assess their great need for better emotional health. Most of these men face societal stigmas, lack of financial resources or limited awareness of available support. Attaining access to proper mental health care can increase early intervention and worsen the impact of depression. Addressing the connection between young men, gang affliction and depression requires a multifaceted approach that focuses on addressing the root causes of gang involvement. It will provide accessibility to mental health resources, promoting positive youth development and create opportunities for education and employment. It is possible to help young men break free from the cycle of violence and create a path towards mental well-being by addressing these underlying issues.

Men sometimes cover their chinks by involving themselves in risky behaviors. It is predominantly men in these challenges on television shows taking great physical risks.

It is just another opportunity for us to show the world that we are socially acceptable. We reveal our gym bodies to the world searching for admiration and acceptance from society. We show the world our image of strength in hopes of receiving a favorable reaction from our performance. We convince ourselves that we are the epitome of masculinity. The only problem with this image is the unrealistic definition the world has given masculinity. Yes, we are strong physically, but we have feelings, emotions, and unhealed places within us that should also be considered.

In many cultures men are expected to be strong, independent and in control but most only give the appearance of strength. Some are judged heavily on their appearance, their ability to provide and their successes. This also determines the position within their family, who they marry and their economic status. Pressure is on both the man who has these attributes to always remain on top as well as the man who does not measure up. They are considered a disgrace within the community.

When a chink is revealed in our armor it can threaten our perceived status and determine our reputation. This can create an onset of abnormal behavior. A chink can feel like a powerful villain that we must destroy at any cost because the idea of looking weak is too great of a threat. In this frame of mind to continue the appearance of strength our risk-taking levels can go through the roof. The need to have validation in our lives is crucial to our masculinity, especially within our private circles. So, we will find ways to prove bravery or assertiveness and dominance to compensate for our preconceived stoic status. To regain a sense of worth and confidence a man will go the extra mile in abnormal behavior to overcome them instead of working on the root of these feelings which are usually wavering and unpredictable societal opinions.

For we know that risk taking behavior often stimulates the release of adrenaline, which can provide a temporary sense of excitement, thrill, and euphoria. Some of us men may engage in risky activities to escape our negative emotions associated with our vulnerabilities. It can become an addiction used to reroute and distract your feelings by providing a temporary sense of relief or satisfaction.

The Attraction to Distraction

Most young men love sports, specifically basketball. Now imagine being a young man who has a lot of friends that also love the game but out of all of them you are the worst player. You would feel insecure anytime you played the game, and we know you would be the target of unmeasurable trash talk. As a young man in this situation, how would you distract yourself from these feelings? How would you handle feeling like an outsider who is ashamed and ridiculed? Anxiety and low self-esteem would cause a reaction that could either trigger the onset of depression or put you on a path of self-acceptance.

Finding chinks in your armor such as low self-esteem will have you question your worth and show the origin of how you allow others to treat you. How do we stop these feelings from creating a domino effect in our lives. I asked a few men what they considered to be a chink in their armor. Their answers varied from anxiety from being a first-time dad, sexual insecurities, trust issues because of childhood trauma, inconsistency with keeping a job and paying the bills. It is safe to say that most of us men walk around in life carrying self-disapprovals over issues that could be resolved if only we were more expressive and less judgmental of each other and ourselves. If only we did not sign on to the the theory that men cannot help other men unless there is a hidden agenda. If only we would be honest with ourselves. The same things we ridicule each other about are the same things we all suffer from.

We find ways of exuding a fake superiority towards each other but through this falsehood of superiority truth always reveals itself.

Pornography the Secret and Shameful Chink.

Pornography addiction stems deeper than sexual desires and fantasy. It is a distraction from your current situation. It is as a means of escape from negative emotions, life stressors and possible sexual assault. However, like any other distraction, relying on pornography to help you cope with these emotions can create shame and guilt once revealed. Dissatisfaction with self can contribute to the development of depressive symptoms. It is an invisible chink that does not become a problem until it becomes uncontrollable. Pornography often presents a distorted idealized version of sexual experiences and body images. Extreme exposure to these unrealistic and contorted portrayals can lead to a discrepancy within a man's reality involving women.

Pornography has tricked many men with undiagnosed mental struggles into merging this fantasy and money driven industry within their real life. Men who perform sexual attacks toward women often indulge in this activity. These sexual scenes quickly become their indulgences. Men who commit these crimes suffer from delusional disorder. This is when a man does not distinguish the difference between reality and fantasy. His mental disorder can originate from severe depression especially if the person is using drugs and alcohol and experiencing hallucinations and delusional thoughts.

Excessive consumption of pornography may lead to relationship problems. As a man when we are dissatisfied within our intimate relationship, we seek satisfaction elsewhere. Because we do not want to cause more problems at home nor do we want to talk about it, we justify our actions by emotionally holding our partner responsible for our actions. In this regard, this behavior will decrease intimacy, communication difficulties occur, and the production unrealistic expectations of your partner increases. This issue becomes a problem when it leads to distance between you and your spouse and family. We also begin to lose interest in our partner intimately or try to force our warped fantasy upon them. Unfortunately, this state of mind increases volatile sexual crimes against women because our sense of reality is blurred by delusion. The victim becomes a conquest and is no longer a human.

Those of us who are not married or in a committed relationship, look for women who are identical to the women in these movies. We look and assume that all women we encounter are similar to them. The perfect woman. These women do not need respect or flirting; you do not have to prove yourself to them, you do not have to meet any societal requirements to get what you really want from them. Their bodies are always considered available for our basic primal needs. It's sex without any work involved but when you question your reason for entertaining yourself in this manner the truth will surface. Are we looking for perfection, companionship or are we attracted to a distraction? Is this distracting us from more substantial and deeper healing? Is this purely entertaining or am I fooling myself and creating an addiction that will warp my image of women? Answer those questions honestly without any deflection on anyone else.

Another aspect of this type of distraction is that it can convince us men to view women as sexual objects therefore erasing the chances of rejection. Controlling the feeling of rejection prevents you from allowing the other person the opportunity to judge you. It builds an imaginary wall around yourself, in this case, removing the victim's right to say no. In these types of situations everything is superficial, which is something the world thrives on.

Whether your chink is societal or personal, chinks can change the feelings you have about yourself. Start with how you see yourself, not as the world views you. Real change requires real work, real accountability, and real discipline. This one is personal for me. For me to have the things I dreamed of and have talked about for years, I had to stop dreaming and stop talking. I put in the work, the discipline and I focused on the end game. I had to hold myself accountable for not being where I knew I should have been years ago.

Functioning with Chinks

Chinks show our human frailty, but it does not have to define it. Do not allow the chinks in your armor to defeat you or your purpose in life. You are more than your shortcomings. You can overcome them and be a better version of yourself. However, if they are affecting your life so that you cannot function properly, take control by seeking help. Be honest with yourself and ask challenging questions. Am I happier with or without it? Is it destroying my relationships, my family, my career, my spiritual life, my goals, and my dreams? Is it a distraction? How did it begin? Why can't I stop? Why haven't I stopped?

Know that chinks in your armor do not define your strength nor your promise. It is important to note that everyone's reaction to discovering weaknesses or chinks in their armor can be different and difficult to accept. Some men may become introspective and determined not to address this part of themself by denying it, but this tactic always leads to a man succumbing to it at some point in their life.

How and when a man reacts to his chinks depends on his individual personality, mindset, and his support system.

Be motivated to improve yourself and set clear goals for yourself. They must be goals that are reachable. If obesity is something that you are suffering with. Make decisions to work out at least once a week. If insecurity is something that you are suffering with, encouraging posts left around the house can help. Make sure that every day you say something positive to yourself. If anxiety is something that troubles you, learn meditation. Give yourself a moment every day to breathe deeply and relax yourself. If you are dealing with rage and anger issues, find something that makes you smile, something that makes you laugh. Make small steps in the beginning and breakdown larger goals into smaller manageable tasks.

Ask yourself why you want to improve yourself. What is it in your life you want to change? What drives you to wanting better? What are the benefits for you being better? Put a plan together and imagine yourself healthier and happier. Keep that picture in your mind even if you make a mistake. Do not beat yourself up if you fall, get back up dust yourself off and keep going. Continue to see the success that you will be if you keep going. Allow that to reinforce you every time you want to give up.

Surround yourself with people who want the best for you. If that is not in your inner circle there are support groups that can give you the emotional encouragement you need. Unfortunately, some of the people closest to us were the most damaged. Their connection to us is the source of our vulnerability. Sometimes our biggest supporters are people we do not know. Strangers have motivated me more than you know. While you are growing, and your mind is changing embrace the new and improved you. Be aware that change may require the ending of some friendships, relationships, and fellowships. It may hurt in the beginning but if there is a connection to any toxicity that could cause you to pause your growth in any way it is worth letting go.

Keep track of your progress. Keep a journal, a whiteboard, even notes to inspire yourself to keep going. Another thing that will keep you on your toes is having someone to hold you accountable for the goals you are trying to reach. Have someone in your life, a coworker, a relative, anyone that you trust to be there when you need guidance. Someone that will celebrate your accomplishments with you.

Reward yourself when you reach a certain milestone. Celebrate your journey because this will give you a positive mindset about your journey, especially when the negative self-talk begins to taunt you. Most of all be kind to yourself. Change your mindset, it's not an easy task. But it is a worthy task. Changing your habits and lifestyle is not easy either, but well worth the outcome. The goal is not to eliminate every chink in your armor. The goal is to remove everything that sets you back and stops you from living your best life. The goal is to be happy with yourself. Recommit to yourself every time you have a setback. Refocus on your goals that you have made for yourself. Be patient with yourself and enjoy your journey of self-improvement.

Take those chinks in your armor and repurpose them. Turn them into wisdom to instruct the next man and the next man that you can overcome and live your life to the fullest.

The Journey of Restoration

Embracing Healing and Finding Completeness

Chapter 6

Going from Brokenness to Wholeness

"It is easier to build strong children than to repair broken men." Frederick Douglas

A broken man in a world full of blind people seems normal because he looks like everyone else. No one notices him. They have no concern as this broken man makes his way around. He is seen every day in the same area as the mob of people rushing past him. Back and forth all day walking pass him, sometimes stepping over him with occupied minds and completely oblivious to the pain around them. His back aches, his clothes are dirty, and his shoes are busted but he is not concerned about his appearance. In his mind he looks like everyone else. He has been on the street for years; he has stopped worrying about time because it is not essential anymore. He has a small tent that houses all his valuables. They are tucked away in a corner far away from the sidewalk. This is home for him. The world has been harsh, and life has broken him.

Unfortunately, this intro can describe so many homeless men broken and battered by our society and by life. When using the term, "broken man," it usually describes a man who is emotionally and psychologically struggling with unhealed traumas. The symptoms vary but the common signs are usually the same.

Men and Emotional Brokenness

 Men experiencing physical and emotional trauma such as losing a loved one or even a significant life-threatening event can deeply change a man's emotional well-being. These events can shatter a man's sense of stability, his peace of mind and cause him to develop PTSD. Men experiencing difficulties in relationships such as breakups, divorces or conflicts with family and friends eventually show emotional stress mainly because of their inability to express their feelings. The inability to converse about their feelings causes distress and can leave a man feeling defeated.

Relationship issues can lead to feelings of rejection, betrayal, loneliness, and a loss of connection and support. Men feel frustration when facing setbacks from job losses or if they are having difficulties in achieving a professional goal. These all can have a profound impact on a man's self-esteem and his identity. He will begin to feel unfulfilled and unsuccessful in his career. This can contribute to him having a sense of purposelessness. Many men are suffering from untreated mental health conditions because of these factors. They are unknown because of his silence.

The Invisible Societal Hand over his Mouth

The silence among men is one of the major components to his failing mental health. We are more prone to anxiety, post-traumatic stress disorder, and substance abuse because we fear our masculinity will be challenged. It also affects how we handle our daily life stressors which support our family's livelihood, our own personal feelings, our health and even our spiritual life.

 Without positive encouragement to express themselves a pressure begins to build within him that causes him to shut down even more. This overload of inner pressure contributes to his vulnerability and detachment from his own emotions resulting in a man's increased inability to connect on an emotional level with anyone.

Some of us experience childhood abuse and neglect or other forms of trauma that take root and linger longer in our lives because they have not been processed in a healthy way. Instead, these unresolved traumas can lead to emotional brokenness, as it may manifest in countless ways, such as trust issues, low self-esteem, or difficulty forming healthy relationships.

The Shield of Masculinity

The world expects men to embody the look of strength and to be the model of endurance. We are liable to endure pain without showing any expression of discomfort. We live within this rough terrain of emotionless life everyday of our lives. It is so saturated within us that it feels uncomfortable and awkward to not be in control of our feelings. However, underneath this rough terrain of emotions and masculinity there are feelings, worries and concerns just like any other person. We are complex and complicated human beings and though we try to come across as simplistic it's always exposed. We carry a sense of pride deeply rooted within us. When we are perceived as incompetent and unintelligent about matters in our life we feel like failures. All of this occurs without one word spoken.

We blame women for sending mixed signals but to be honest we do as well. We are experts at agreeing to something we do not want to do or go along with something because we will not vocalize what we really want or how we really feel. For example, when we see a beautiful woman and we want to get her attention we will muster up our courage and approach her not knowing what the response will be. We can throw our best line at her and still feel rejected. At this moment, we must have the self-esteem to walk away from that situation without feeling rejected and/or angry. Society expects us to swallow our pride and walk away from that situation as if nothing happened at all.

For the woman, the event is over but for the man living with depression or any mental struggle it can trigger a dormant level of emotions and unwelcoming behavior. Because of our ability to hold on to traumatic situations that could date back to our childhood the last straw can be explosive. Let's face it guys, some of us cannot handle social rejection because we secretly reject ourselves and we are looking for acceptance from others.

Burdens of Expectations

Roles within the genders are as important now as they have been in over 50 years. Though with each generation the roles slightly change. Yet the mental standing of man's emotional health has plummeted due to the lack of empathy regarding it. In this modern way of masculinity men are expected to be more compassionate and even empathetic in their lifestyle and choices. However, our roles of breadwinners, leaders, and protectors are prevalent. In many cultures the man is the dominant figure within the home and the family financially. But along with this comes the pressure of society's heavy expectations.

Our identity as a man is formed along the lines of our success or failure. Despite the forces against us we are to be successful, the breadwinner and the protector.

The societal finger wag happens to any man who falls short of success. The demand can cause men to make work and money more important than anything else even themselves. Because of this we tie our success to our self-worth. We take on the ideals of the world of what is worth and what is not. Our relationships stop being a priority and begin to suffer because our focus is on earning more money. But how did he end up here? After about an hour I learned so much about this man. He is an army veteran, father of four, what happens when we do not meet societal expectations? What happens when we fail? How do we handle losing control? The world has no empathy for those who are not successful. This is proven by the plethora of homeless and poverty-stricken people in our country alone. There's not enough empathy in our society to combat the merciless and uncaring manner of our systems.

This brings us back to the man in the intro of this chapter who sleeps on the street. A variety of things happened for him to end up in this predicament. He decided to withdraw from society and isolate himself in his own world. Therefore, establishing his own rules, and his own happiness for his life. In his mind, he is escaping what broke him, but it has imprisoned him within invisible bars.

You may ask him what brought him to this reality. He was not always this way.

Meet Charles

Having random conversations with people is nothing new for me, but I saw Charles sitting against a corner store gazing out at the people. I introduced myself and offered him lunch. We talked about the book but suddenly the topic switched to his life and how he identified with the cover.

One thing I know about us men, we have the best conversation over some delicious food, drinks, and sports. I did not want to pry into his personal life, but I had to know college educated man who lost his wife after 47 years of marriage. I walked away realizing that the dirty clothes, the uncombed hair, the lowered gaze was what he wrapped himself in to distance himself from the rest of the world. He created his own little cocoon. No one would come close enough to see the cracks, the man entrapped in his own misery.

Charles was married 47 wonderful years to whom he referred to as my BFF. No one knew me or loved me like she did. Unfortunately, his beloved wife died slowly from breast cancer. He spent every dime he had on doctors, medicine, and medical bills. They met in grammar school and were inseparable. She was his whole life. But when she lost her battle to cancer, he lost his will to go on. He told me of the last time he was at the family house. His children had all moved out and begun living their own lives. He and his wife were finally empty nesters making plans for their future when cancer disrupted their plans. He left letters to all the kids, divided the money four ways, left the keys to the vehicles along with the house keys and walked away. He never returned. He was broken.

How many of us can connect with his story? There are many things in this world that can break us as men. Losing someone this close to you can indeed break your heart and in his case it becomes unbearable. Life became unbearable.

This makes me think of the saying, hurt people hurt people. You may wonder how he hurt anyone, but you must consider that he left his children as well. His pain went from his own heart ache to his children who need their dad despite their ages. It was a loss for the entire family. To this day he carries guilt for not saving her life. He blames himself for not giving her better care she so desperately needed. He punishes himself with isolation and withdrawal from society, his family, and the new generations within his family.

Charles does not see any way out of the prison he created for himself, and he does not want to. He is metaphorically a broken man.

The Many Faces of Brokenness

Many men fit the description of brokenness but master the art of covering it up. It is clear in their self-esteem, low self-worth, no motivation, and persistent sadness. They dwell in a low place every day. But there are other sides of brokenness that are often overlooked. There is aggression driven brokenness. Those who experience brokenness in their youth grow to form hostile feelings towards anything that triggers the source of this feeling. These men are susceptible to violence. Violence becomes an avenue they choose to live on, unleashing their feelings upon those they consider weak. They find power in preying upon those that remind them of the time they were innocent. Thoughts run through their minds of when the offense was upon them and created the monster that remains. The mental justification of abusing others causes an elevation of attacks every time.

A broken man's aggression does not always have to be volatile. It can also be in sports assertiveness and among his peers. They usually have an overly competitive approach to winning. Unusually competitive ways that are combined with berating their opponents is another sign of aggression. We have all met that guy or we are that guy. He is the one that has all the friends that hang with him, but they only tolerate him because he exudes societal power. The world determines power by how many people you bring fear upon, the amount of control you have and the lack of empathy towards others as you manipulate your way to the top. These men always have a flock of mediocre men around him to make him feel stronger. He gives the others a false sense of protection. He also gives them a sense of belonging. This may sound like a high school mindset, but you would be surprised how this becomes a lifestyle for some of us who feel as if we peaked in those times.

The leader of this pact personality is formed while in adolescence. The bully character existed mainly to hide and protect his trauma and ego. The first insult happened by someone he trusted. Another reason for this character is to protect himself by switching places with the bully at home or in his past. It is very possible that this young man admired the man that had control over weakness. He looks powerful. At the same time, however, he hates himself for being weak and easily preyed upon. He becomes the predator but the more the predator evolves, the more the hurt child is revealed.

This behavior also lingers on to his relationships. Have you ever met people in your life who do not seem to change for the better? They have not grown mentally, emotionally, or maturely. They are the same as they were when you were all children. It is as if they are stuck in time. Their bodies have grown, their hair has turned grey, but their conversation remains the same. The child inside has remained and has taken over their life. This man has not done much with himself. He has not left the area he grew up in. He is now someone's father but only by name. For this man to leave his childhood he will have to address what has stunted his emotional growth. The distressing events that occurred in his childhood have held him hostage in his adulthood and are presently emotionally causing him to still be frozen in time.

To change the face of brokenness one must adopt forgiveness. Embracing forgiveness is the means of breaking the curse from your life. Without this most necessary part to healing, you will at some point in your life repeat the same abuse in your adulthood. You will hurt someone in the same manner or worse. Most are not aware that they are repeating this cycle of dysfunction by creating excuses for their injurious behavior. Sometimes all it takes is someone outside of their circle to compare their behavior to someone else in their past for them to see this pattern.

The curse of brokenness begins to trickle down the bloodline hitting every generation of men and scarring the women as well. Brokenness exposes generational lies, abuse, fights, deep dark secrets, mental illnesses and so much more. The innocent children within the family fall victim to them all. This has happened and continues to happen within our families until it has become the responsibility of this generation to choose to help the family heal or walk away from the family that they love due to their toxic ways for their own mental well-being.

Then there is the functioning broken man. He worries me the most. The façade he has is perfect. He keeps his finances right; he stays at the gym, and he is well mannered and well spoken. He always has a romantic partner. He is the epitome of a perfect mate. Unbeknownst to most he has deep emotional trauma that he avoids. He reminds me of a great escape artist.

The Runner

This man has learned from his past to keep certain things about himself undercover. He has not healed he just learned the art of covering up his true identity. He has an enormous fear of poverty, and this makes him work harder and longer than anyone else. His aim is to continue to climb that corporate ladder until everyone is underneath him. The Runner does not care who he hurts and betrays to get to the top. But even with all the ambition and successes he is still not happy. He could also be the nicest person until a certain trigger is activated then a completely different side of him will surface. This man only shows his true colors if his emotional wall is crumbling. Broken men reveal themselves whether voluntarily or involuntarily. When it does it shocks everyone who thought they knew him best.

Brokenness has exposed me many times. I once had an addiction to pornography during one of the most stressful points of my life. At first, it was a great escape from my world's pressures, but that began to change. I have always had the upmost respect for women and never would treat them in any ill-mannered way. But I noticed that my thoughts of them were becoming more sexual and more objective. My routine had even changed. I would go to work, race home to grab a beverage and turn on my favorite escape. I turned the rest of the world off and gave it all my attention. I remember the day I realized that I had a problem with pornography. I was on the train staring at this woman I did not know, allowing my imagination to take over. Our eyes met and I felt as if she knew what I was thinking. I turned away from her ashamed and in disbelief that these scenes had taken over my mind in such a brief time. But despite the embarrassment of that situation, I continued to watch them. I knew then I had a problem, which was the last thing I needed. I began to question why

I began watching it in the first place. How was it helping me? It became a daily activity that I could not seem to stop. I had a new fight on my hands, addiction.

Addiction is a compulsive habit-forming substance or action that may produce negative withdrawal symptoms. I was not happy in my life; this gave me short term pleasure with long-term negative effects. Feeling ashamed of the way I was handling my life caused me to go into a deeper depression. The mind can be fragile yet powerful regarding its wants and desires. Depression has a negative effect on our cognitive thinking and combining this with fantasy can be a lethal mixture to our journey by causing more damage and making it harder to achieve mental health. There are too many cases of men who are struggling mentally that use addiction to dull their memories of trauma that are now living with a blurred line of reality and fantasy. I know this reality all too well. I too was broken and like any other man searched for escapism instead of help.

We all agree that escaping can be a lot easier than seeking help. In fact, we find looking and asking for help embarrassing. Everyone knows a man would rather get lost than ask for directions. Even if it means driving up and down the same road until we figure it out. Why don't we have the same mindset when it comes to our mental health? We turn to addictions and distractions hoping that it will take our minds off our troubles. We are creating contrary methods of dealing with our mental struggles that are not accommodating our goals. These methods are tricking our minds into believing that we can finally enjoy something that will take the pain away.

We try to immerse ourselves into activities that give us temporary relief but overall, we realize that we were wasting time and energy.

After trying to distract myself I understood that my time could have been used better. I should have been working on a business plan, working on my diet, authoring this book, repairing the breakage within family, and managing my money better. My reality proved to me that the real reason I was engulfed in this distraction was because I was lonely and wanted love, wanted someone to validate me and most importantly, I wanted to stop hurting.

Breaking Free

Removing the broken chains will take work. This may be the understatement of the year but nevertheless it does not make it anymore truer. Who is more deserving of finally having positive mental health than you? No one. How can your family function properly if the head of the family is emotionally healthy? You are a man, but you are human first. Your mental health is as important if not more important than your physical health. We come from all social classes, diverse cultures, and backgrounds but there is one thing we men all have in common; we deserve to be emotionally healthy and healed from our past traumas. We are not cut from the same cloth, but we are made in his image. We deserve to be free to be our authentic self and change the way the world defines us.

Striving for Wholeness

Let us make walking in our wholeness normal but how do we become whole. Let's first give our minds over to being whole by determining what it entails and how it is achieved. We should first start with overriding societal norms, stereotypes, and expectations. The stereotype that men lack masculinity if they display any vulnerable emotion is not only untrue but has caused extreme emotional damage to generations of men.

Societal norm that men should be the sole breadwinner in the household. I believe this decision can be made within the family. The weight should not be solely on the man unless circumstances call for it. The expectation of man is people expecting us to always show assertiveness and independence regardless of our life's situations. This expectation is hugely unrealistic yet expected and demanded. Our society marvels at the look of success, frowning upon anything less than.

Men have the power to change the definition of man without giving the belief of weakness. Men are capable of being strong in the weakness moments of their lives. My wife always tells me that a man in touch with his feelings is a man displaying immovable power. He is in control of his emotions, and this will enrich his masculinity. Having the ability to interact with the often side of yourself while balancing the stronger side takes skill and a well-rehearsed balancing act. It's something that should have been taught by our fathers. This is a normalcy not granted to many.

This must be a change each man takes upon himself. Society will never approve of such a change because it would prove that they were in error from the beginning.

The world would rather we portray the unbreakable image of a man whether it is false is of no concern. They would criticize and label us before admitting that the emotional turmoil men suffer from is a direct connection to the unwritten rule we must live by in our personal lives.

We have the power to rewrite these rules that were initially written by men who wanted more than anything to separate the genders. The goal was always to put a defining line between us therefore the concept of women being the weaker sex was born. The idea was that a woman would always need a man to help her, make the decisions and protect them. These men felt the need for superiority over women as their way of showing masculinity. This mindset was toxic and still reigns strongly within our cultures.

Though the world enforces this type of masculinity our inner circles are guilty of the same. Men are not known for giving each other grace for looking weak. We are harder on each other than any woman. That is because we are aware of how hard this world is on the weak. They do not not survive. They are succumbed. Let us change the narrative by reinforcing mental health in schools targeting our young men who are displaying emotional struggles at an early age. Normalizing family therapy when emotional trauma is evident within the generations. Address the issues within our families and eliminate the fear of healing. This is the main goal, removing the deadly fear factor and expose the problems.

Layers of Man

All men have faith even if its minuscule. There is a place in all of us that holds all our secrets and conversations we have had within ourselves. The part of us we do not share with anyone. In this hidden place the younger version of us exists. The uncertain teenager that had no direction lives there. The adult man who remains uncertain about matters from his childhood was birthed from here.

 He remains in a pattern he witnessed from other men and assumes that it is the norm though he is still unsure of it. Nevertheless, he has faith and hope that one day he can finally be in a safe place emotionally and finally be doubt free. Within himself is a small possibility that he can one day be free and live in the full spectrum of his humanity by accepting his flaws and insecurities. Acknowledging and accepting that he blazes his own path and that he is not nor needs to be a carbon copy of anyone else. He does not have to carry anyone else's guilt for acts done to him. He is free from guilt though he was unable to protect others who were victimized. He had no control over their trauma. He can allow the predators of his youth to carry their own shame and guilt. They are responsible for their own actions. Break free and forgive yourself. Forgive those who hurt you and start living your life independently from depression.

Purpose in Pain

Find support. We all need support. All human beings need something or someone that gives us the feeling of support. Even though some of us prefer solitude from people. Their preference is pets or remote locations. This is helpful as well. The focus is to be in a safe place that makes you feel at peace. Support is where you can release without judgement or shame.

My support was prayer and meditation. This was my support. Praying in solitude helps me release my anxieties and frustrations. It helps me remove the burdens from my mind and brings me a source of relief. As my prayer life increased the ability to mourn my parents for the first time since their transition arose. My parents died 8 months apart from each other and in that same year I was in the middle of divorce proceedings. During this time prayer and meditation allowed me to mourn all my broken relationships and bad decisions.

Prayer and meditation allowed me to process my negative traits. It helped me to understand the sources of my inconsistencies toward myself and my children. I was also able to dwell on my disapproval of myself. I hated the weight I gained and the traps that I fell for in my life. I was tired of being taken for granted by people. I had to learn to stand up for myself and exercise the word "No" for my own peace of mind. The purpose of this was to let myself go through the process and become better for it. I planned to take steps towards improvement and never look back.

Gentlemen, it is necessary to find solace in our pursuit of wholeness. Prayer and meditation helped me however, if this does not work for you there are many other avenues you can explore such as private therapy, mental health centers, family therapy or a men's community group. As you heal find activities that give you joy, something to look forward to. Whether it be creative expression, mentoring at a boy's club or even aiding senior citizens. Be of service to others and you will find purpose for your life.

Discover who you are without the painful memories. Transform yourself into who you choose to be not who you were damaged into becoming. No one was born damaged; it took an act of hate in your life to create this person. There was once an earlier version of you, now you have the power and authority to change for a better version you never thought you could be. Some of you may feel that the pieces of the chains are too scattered to be put back together. You could not be more wrong. No one is beyond repair. No one is beyond forgiveness. Every man deserves self-compassion.

Therefore, cultivate higher self-esteem and motivate others to do the same. Embark on this new journey to wholeness. You will be setting a new narrative for masculinity, healing of yourself, forgiving others, erasing old trauma that once had a hold on you mentally and physically. Accept your flaws, overcome your insecurities, find purpose, and meaning for your life. Show the proof that men can navigate through their journey with authenticity.

The journey from brokenness to wholeness is an ultra-personal one. Every journey is different, but they all have one goal and that's transformation.

Shedding the Weight

Embracing Forgiveness and Self Compassion

Chapter 7

Removing Shame and Guilt

"Within the depths of shame and guilt, men hold the power to transform their pain into resilience, their mistakes into lessons, and their past into a catalyst for growth."

Shame and guilt are two issues every man confronts at every stage of his life. Men associate shame with a weakness of character. So of course, we will do whatever it takes to avoid it. It is a constant reminder of a failure or something we did not have any experience of. We are initially unaware of the possibility that shame and guilt over time could burrow within us causing it to connect to our personality. The telltale sign of this happening is a statement like, "I'm just being me."

Trigger Me Trauma

Remember guys, the very offense we are guilty of has been festering within us for years now. Past shameful offenses that are unhealed normally drill their way into our present psyche. This in effect changes our normal dispositions and affects our temperament. It also causes us to be on edge most of the time, considering the triggers involved. Triggers are anything that conjures bad memories of past trauma. Anything that causes us to relive negative experiences. It could be anything from a scent, a person or even a sensitive subject.

Triggers can vary from person to person but there are some that are just more common among men. There are a few triggers that all men deal with such as difficulties in relationships. Common difficulties in our relationships are any type of conflict, breakups, or loss of a loved one.

These can trigger a man and contribute to their feelings of depression. Elevated levels of stress due to work can be a daily trigger for men.

Factors like job dissatisfaction, or unemployment can be triggers for depression amongst men. More factors such as job expectations, pressure to meet expectations, working long hours or facing job insecurities can take a toll on a man's mental health.

On a personal note, the very idea of not having enough money to support myself and my family can send me spiraling. I know I am not alone in that feeling. Financial problems, such as debt, financial insecurities or job loss can lead to significant stress levels in a man. The answer is to figure out what triggers you negatively and release yourselves from its influence. Though this may seem easier said than done, releasing yourself from the emotional ties to money will help us strategies our managing of it.

Shame On Us All

Shame is a complex emotion that can vary from person to person. Every one of us has done shameful things but we do not all feel the same about them. While it is not possible to pinpoint one specific thing all men might find shameful. There are some examples that are common within all men such as past mistakes, failures, personal shortcomings, or actions that may have hurt people that we care about. All these factors can produce shame however, chronic feelings of shame can eventually bring an onset of depression.

 To remove shame and guilt we must first have the courage to look in the mirror. We must hold ourselves accountable for our part in the offense. I know this all too well. I am sure you all can relate to it as well. We pretend as if the offense never happened. We hope everyone involved has forgotten or we lose contact with them. Fooling ourselves into thinking that the incident will fade away. We must face our shame head on by digging up those past hurts no matter how deep or painful.

The first step to removing shame and guilt is excepting your part in the event. Ask yourself this important question. Why did I do this? Answer in complete honesty. Look in the mirror and see your own reflection. Do not make any excuses and do not pass any judgement on yourself. Reflect in that moment and except your reason for your actions. For some of us that will be our first time showing responsibility for something we have done as well as something we have been avoiding for years.

Without this first step, your mind will take the details of this event and inevitably disorganize the scenes in which you took part. Our minds are powerful. We have the power to remove ourselves or justify our own wrongdoings. Without accountability the guilt will continue to taunt you until you suppress it more and unknowingly act out your guilt upon someone innocent. Your mind could begin to exaggerate parts or find fault with someone else who thought you were guilty. Creating the delusion that you are innocent while spreading untruths.

Our brains can trick us in many ways. However, it affects you and unavoidably someone else. It will cause more damage to you and not only yourself but to all your relationships.

Digging Down to the Root of It

Men can experience something like relational trauma. They enter a new relationship and begin to express old thoughts, or details from earlier relationships in which they were accused of shameful acts. If the first offense was within a personal relationship, guilt will cause anxiety of repeating the offense therefore preventing you from future happiness with someone you love.

Fear of accountability causes you to repeat past offenses. For example, abusive traits, becoming non communicative or displaying possessiveness towards your partner. If this is the case, find someone to converse with. Whether it is a friend, a relative or a professional. Find a trusted person and free yourself from every detail. Without this necessary step the guilt will eventually break you down. Unfortunately, hurting people, hurt people, whether consciously or unconsciously.

This brings us to a deeper area of shame which is psychological trauma. Men who have experienced abuse of sexual assault may develop symptoms of post-traumatic stress disorder PTSD. This brings upon intrusive memories, flashbacks, nightmares, or even hyper-vigilance. They may also experience anxiety and fear and a sense of helplessness. Men who survived abuse or any sexual assault often experience wider ranges of emotions. Their shame and guilt can mix with anger, even sadness and this mixture of emotions will show within their behavior. Unfortunately, sexual assault according to society, is more of gender-based offense.

Gender-based offenses can be initiated by a person or group of people whose main objective is to violate someone unethically. Gender-based offenses, however, are discriminatory and violent only to a specific gender. There are more assaults including sexual assaults towards women than men. Nevertheless, men are victims of abuse and sexual assault more so than not. The reason the statistics are not well known about these cases is because men who are victims of this crime do not confess it.

Men face other challenges due to societal expectations surrounding masculinity, which can make it difficult to express and process these emotions. These pent-up emotions that men are not allowed to express at times can become evident in their relationships. The trauma of abuse and sexual assault can affect an individual's ability to trust others and form healthy relationships. We may struggle with intimacy and experience difficulties setting up emotional connections due to this inability. These men show avoidance behavior to protect themselves. This behavior is deeply rooted in societal definitions and acceptance of offenses concerning certain genders.

In this case, society only accepts women to be victims of sexual harassment, assaults, stalking and power imbalance. Gender based offenses perpetuate inequality which is solely because of men domination. This is primarily the reason male sexual assaults are ignored or not taken seriously.

Men living with depression may also turn to substance abuse or engage in self-destructive behavior. When we are looking for coping mechanisms for our trauma the embarrassment of it all keeps us quiet. These behaviors can serve as a temporary escape from the shame that we feel.

No man enjoys the feeling of being powerless. The stigma associated with being a male survivor of any type of sexual assault can further contribute to the development of depression.

Process of Removal

Forgive yourself and accept your mistakes. Mistakes do not define your worth. Shame can emasculate a man. We all have flaws. Perfection may be what some strive for but it's unrealistic. For this very reason men internalize shame brought about by societal messages that associate mistakes or wrongdoings with weakness or lack of masculinity. To error is human, however hiding from it is acceptable and encouraged in our society. It is acceptable in our society to put upon the image of perfection yet live in lack. It is unfortunate that a lot of us feel that we have no choice but to live this way because of the way our system is set up.

Impractical roles of a man in this world do not include asking for forgiveness or showing any concern for healing. We have been taught not to show emotion while pretending to be hard and uncaring. A learnt behavior that eventually hurts us and those we lose in the end. I challenge your negative behavior and society's expectations that may hinder self-forgiveness. Recognize that being vulnerable, making mistakes and giving yourself grace are signs of strength and courage. I have counseled men who battle with forgiveness. The struggle was how the public would perceive them. We were taught that a man should never have to ask for forgiveness because it was thought of as feminine. However, we learn later that lack of grace is a road to depression.

Guys, it starts with you. Before you can ask for forgiveness, you must forgive yourself. I remember a time I was married in the past. We were in those awkward moments toward the end when the feeling of failure took over me. It was my second marriage to end in divorce. I felt as if I had not done enough in this marriage as the man. It was a personal and public scar for me that I could not escape. It took years for me to forgive myself for the role I played in its demise. It also took time for me to let go of the psychological weight that did not belong to me. I am on the other side of guilt and now I am walking in my healing.

I have concluded that being a man carries a vast number of expectations beginning from birth. Once you are assigned as a male at the start of your life, you are instantly given responsibility and preconceived notations of how you should live, act, and conduct yourself as a man. You are expected to take upon a mantle. In my case, I was given my father's name.

It was not until I was a man and had my own son that I realized the responsibility of that honor and the expectations he had looking down at his infant son. I now understand.

Nevertheless, alongside having two failed marriages, not carrying out my dreams or achieving my goals, I slipped into depression. The shame that comes from failing can send a man into a head spin. Failure very seldom happens without an audience. My family and friends were watching my life plummet.

My children were watching and were extremely disappointed in me. Mostly I was disappointed in myself. Failure felt like an itchy suit of ants crawling all over my skin tormenting me day and night.

I have always been a laid-back guy but during this time of my life I did not recognize myself. You know that moment when as a man is looking for something, anything to take the pain away. You become desperate in the search for a moment you can step out of that world and be somewhere else. To be honest, given the choice of fight or flight, I was out of there. I took on different jobs and began to start drinking heavily. I tried trips and gifts to reconcile my marriage at the time but to no avail. I could not figure it out, so like most of us, I turned to escaping my reality which was an incredibly low point. I hit rock bottom.

My life was upside down. Though I was still working and still functioning. I was depressed and incredibly unhappy with myself and my life. I understand now that depression looks different for each of us. The shame that covered me like a blanket and the guilt I felt inside became apparent in my weight gain, my temperament, and my parenting. Flight was my way of coping with my shame. Even if I was physically present, I was emotionally absent. I removed myself from the very things that meant the most to me.

Guilt was plaguing my life and overwhelmed me as it has so many other men. I realized during that time that people will always remind you of your failures and never of your successes. You will always be reminded how you handled things and often given unsolicited advice.

Furthermore, intensify your frustration. I sought after quick fixes instead of permanent resolutions. The anxiety that came with my shame and guilt would not allow me to sit and think, it made me run in search of instant satisfaction.

Most men look for the uncomplicated way out of involving themselves in emotional trauma. Digging deep into our emotions is not one of our favorite activities. It is usually something we avoid at all costs. To us it takes up too much time to dig up things that happened long ago. It is a waste of time. We would rather play sports until we are too tired to talk about it. Our gps somehow reroutes us to the nearest lounge or sports bar instead of home where we must face our feelings and our family's disappointment in us. We become bombarded with extra curricula activities hint hint, that will further damage an already delicate situation. To put it short, we will make matters worse by avoiding it.

This quote has been around since the beginning of time, *"Men and women are complete opposites."* In this regard, it's certainly true. Women have the gift of expression. They can articulate their feelings verbally and emotionally. Men stay silent in fear that no one witnesses their voice shake or crack. To prevent this, we stay quiet, but our actions and behaviors become sirens. Our body language and physical gestures show through our muscles tensing and our teeth gritting but never vocalizing them. Convening our thoughts in a healthy way requires trust and a feeling of safety for us to open up. This is hard to find and even harder to admit. Because of this you will find us fleeing anywhere for distraction.

Sports and men go hand and hand. Physical activity allows us men to express freely and openly with no backlash from society. Most of us find our therapy, our peace and solitude in physical activity. This can be the complete opposite for women. Usually when a man is both verbal and emotional, regarding shame and guilt it results in confrontation which is a defense mechanism. We feel as if we are being forced to talk about something that is too painful to bring up again. We will immediately put our guard up and protect ourselves. Men guard and express their emotions, physically.

Men must learn self-grace. This is why forgiveness of past events starts inside. Men must set their own guidelines for forgiveness of self. We must give ourselves the liberty to become vulnerable and remain masculine. The only place to reach this liberty is by believing that you are a man before, during and after the process of forgiveness. I am still a man, even though I feel shame.

I am still a man even though I feel guilty. I was wrong and it was wrong what happened to me, and I must prevent guilt from tearing me apart mentally.

Without self-grace men also become emotionally immature. Having the inability to work out issues within relationships is just one of the characteristics of emotional immaturity in men. Most men have not learned to forgive because they were not taught. We learn by watching and repeating the behaviors from the men in our life. For some, there were no examples of men behaviors, so they learn from the lack of healthy masculine behavior. In all adolescent environments, a healthy approach to forgiveness will create a more balanced and emotionally stable person.

The signs of a man who is struggling with healing from shame and guilt can be seen in his reactions to rejection. They often display anger and fear when confronted with rejection. We fear being embarrassed or humiliated. Any negative spotlight to attention will bring shame that we all try to avoid. Keeping the persona that we have it all together. The delusion of complete control to avoid looking less than a man.

I have spoken to homeless men who gave up on themselves and the life the pursued because they could not keep up a persona society demanded they have. So, the shame of failing overtook them and they decided to escape and create their own world. They emotionally left this world to seek refuge in another. A gentleman I was counseling who shared that he gave up trying to reconnect with his son due to all the mistakes he made in his childhood.

He did not understand the power of forgiveness. It was not for his son; it was for himself.

Most men do not understand that they have allowed their failures to dominant them. It is like putting yourself at the mercy of another's empathy, which can be very uncomfortable. So, to avoid this they self-medicate with distractions and convince themselves that they do not need healing. We tell ourselves to get over it either from our own voices or others. Most of us try to drown out the loud inner voices of failure with alcohol, drugs, sex and sometimes overworking. Failure accuses you of never doing the right thing or making the right decisions. Guilt will emotionally tie you down in a pool of your own self-doubt until there is no more life left in you.

Grab the reigns of shame and guilt. Take control and understand that the avoidance of your emotions comes from fear. Fear of acknowledging you are not perfect. Fear of allowing your feelings to show up on the outside for all to see. However, if you captured that moment in time, you would see that every man on this planet has experienced it. You are not alone.

Once you have understood the necessity of forgiving yourself, focus on gaining the courage to ask for forgiveness. Lack of this ability casts a look of arrogance. Society may be fond of arrogance, but it only makes it seem as though the person is strong. It proves otherwise. Arrogance gives the appearance of strength, but it shows weakness and a lack of empathy. A prime example of the façade of strength. When we walk toward each other we go through the protocol of the typical man meet. Where we size each other up upon meeting. You know what I mean. That look we give each other. We poke our chest out, heighten our shoulders and walk with more confidence. At least until we have passed the competition. Every male species on the planet does this. That is a little animal planet theory for you.

Why do we do this? To appear strong. To appear as if we have everything under control. Nothing could be further from the truth. But we will never admit it. It must show on the outside what is lacking on the inside. However, in these circumstances, the strength would come from doing the very opposite. If the offense of which you are guilty requires an apology, give the apology. Get the courage to clear the slate.

I got the courage to say I was wrong. I was selfish. I did not think it through, and I should have considered your point of view. As men we love conquering things. When you make it a habit of returning to where you messed up, it becomes easier. You have conquered it.

Consider the benefit of changing the heart of a man by not accepting the status quo of how a man should react to shame and guilt. Let's talk a little more about this.

The Art of Forgiveness

How can men benefit from forgiving themselves and others? The benefit of forgiveness is again not just to the person receiving it but mostly for you. Though my marriage failed I still had to forgive myself for the part I played in its demise. The hardest part for me was apologizing to my children. I had to swallow whatever pride I had left and submit to my children. Apologizing to your children will strengthen the bond between you and them and express the importance of their emotional health.

Forgiveness of self and others is powerful and transformative. For those of us who experienced heightened emotional characteristics like anger. The release of a heaviness like unforgiveness, will lighten the load on your emotions. Take away resentment and replace it with peace. Peace of mind is priceless. It can improve relationships whether romantic, platonic, or future relationships. It is not only women that carry, but we also carry as well. We carry emotionally, traumas that have not healed. We will carry that same pain to a new relationship and make that person a new victim of an old crime.

The main goal of removing shame and guilt is resonance growth. Detach yourself from the trauma whether you were the victim or its cause. This may seem impossible to carry out but the only way to grow is to allow yourself to change for the better. Through this personal growth you will become more aware of self. You will remember the mistakes you made previously and the long-term effect it had on you. You will have learned a new behavior when it comes to conflicts and difficult issues as well as the importance of staying in tune with your emotions.

Emotionally responding in a high conflict moment can lead to saying the wrong things and reverting to an old frame of mind. In this perspective, you will have the opportunity to show empathy and understand what is important. Real growth does not have to be right all the time. Real growth can agree for peace. Agree to discuss it another day. Live in your moment of freedom from the memories that once taunted you. You have the power to change your journey to fight depression brought on through shame and guilt. You took accountability for your actions. There are those that never get to this part. They remain stuck like the homeless men I interviewed for this book. Their lives are frozen in time, and they remain at the mercy of an offense long since passed.

You now understand that the beginning of the journey of removing shame and guilt first starts with you. Forgiving yourself increases empowerment which decreases your chances of depression. It increases chances of better relationships, emotional maturity, and a healthier outlook on life. It eliminates the constant threat of humiliation. You will know that embarrassment is not the lack of masculinity. It does not make you any less of a man.

Remove shame and guilt with eagerness to improve oneself. It will repair broken bridges and give you back time to enjoy life in ways you never have before. Take care of yourself physically and mentally. If you have not already started, eat better and exercise regularly. Make a choice to be happy every day. It can be difficult and may take some practice but it's worth it. Put a reminder on your phone that your happiness matters every day ay yourself to never slip back into that state of mind again.

Renew and rebuild old relationships only if they are nontoxic. Relationships that may have been torn apart because of your past shame and guilt can be repaired but only if the hurt and pain have been uprooted. Make this a priority your mental health is too important. Manage your stress. It is normal to have stress but it's important to manage it correctly. It is also necessary to say that if you need more help with any of these steps do not hesitate to seek professional help. Take the time that you need to become a better version of yourself. Your process to better mental health is as unique as you are.

There are a few ways to cultivate a positive mindset with optimism that may give way to possibility. The possibility of things going the way that you really need them to go. It may not have the exact details that you wanted but the end game will be the same. Realize as you live your life that there are people watching you.

Whether it's your family, children, or friends, there is always someone observing how you navigate your life. You may be inspiring someone else who is losing their grip. By observing your healing process, they could learn that challenges can be opportunities for growth.

I learned that better is usually right around the corner from the hardest fights of your life. Do not allow challenges to overtake you. Do not allow it to succumb your life. Instead walk in your life knowing that there is hope and you will survive this.

A Light in the Darkness
Cultivating Optimism and Possibility

Chapter 8

There Is Hope
"Only in the darkness can you see the stars."

Martin Luther King, Jr.

We may lose many things in our lives, but never lose hope. Losing hope causes you to lose it all to fear. Remaining in a stale state frozen in disparity. Let me repeat, there is hope. The very fact I authored this book proves there is hope. Here's my story.

Fred

I am the middle brother of six kids, so my memories are full of family and friends. My favorite memory is when my younger sister was born on my birthday. I will never forget it. We were having my birthday party, but I knew my mother was going to give birth on my birthday, and I was right. My sister Rene was the best present I could have ever receive. I grew up under the watchful eyes of my parents, older siblings and mostly dominate men. I was disciplined and learned to pray and carry myself in a distinguished way. Time went on and I finally branched out on my own. I began to experience life, love, money, loss of love, advancement, heart ache, then suddenly a serious illness. I relied on the teachings from childhood to carry me through and I still do.

The year 2015 my life began a journey I was not expecting. I have always followed a healthy diet. I loved cigars and API beers but nothing harsh. So, I thought anyway. I noticed I was not feeling the same in my lower region. Of course, as a man I do what we all do and try to ignore it and wish it away. I tried self-remedies, but I was feeling increasingly uncomfortable and then soon the pain became too much to bear. After months of me not taking this too seriously and hoping it would go away, I finally went to the hospital. The doctor prescribed antibiotics and sent me home. I thought this was the cure and my life would quickly go back to normal. It was the complete opposite. I was in for the rollercoaster ride of my life. I was not prepared for what was to come.

This turned into an event I could not wish away or ignore. The pain was getting worse, and I had to do something about it. The antibiotics worked briefly but the pain returned so I went back to the doctor. He could not give me a diagnosis he directed me to a urologist. This scared me to death. I went because I could not take the pain anymore. The doctor checked me and said 2 words that changed my whole life, bladder cancer. He was extremely optimistic and encouraged me the tumor was found early. A biopsy was performed, and I went home with a colostomy bag, which was a nightmare. I was constantly praying that this would be over soon. Nevertheless, I felt like this was the end of this experience and I could put this in my rear-view mirror. However, after this I did what most men do and never followed up with the doctor. The pain stopped and I immediately went back to my old habits. Big mistake.

The fear and uncertainty went away, and I felt like my old self again. I returned to my beers and my favorite cigars hanging out and getting little sleep. 2020 came and I felt amazing. I was single and living my life. However, God had other plans for me. I met this beautiful woman, and we connected on a level I have never experienced before. My life was truly going uphill again. By 2022 those pains returned. I was in total disbelief. This could not happen to me again. So just like before I tried to ignore it and self-medicate the problem but just like before. I had to address it. The pain was a lot more severe and could not have come at a worse time. My girlfriend and I had established a corporation, and we were well on our way to doing important things. It all came to a screeching halt.

We went to the hospital, and they took me in the back to check on me but what happened next is something I will never forget. This scene plays in my mind like an old horror movie. I was sitting in the nursing station, and my girlfriend was sitting across from me. The nurse came and stood between us. She said that she tested all the patients on the floor and there were only two people who had cancer. She looked at both of us and then me and said I am sorry sir; you are one of them. I was in complete shock. I looked at my girlfriend and she had a blank look on her face. It was as if time stood still. I did not notice anything else around me other than her while those words replayed repeatedly in my head. We had plans to get married. We were preparing to move and launch our business. Cancer had taken center stage.

We have talked about this moment so many times. It was the beginning of our union and a rollercoaster road of my health. I recall her mentioning that by saying yes to marrying me meant the possibility of becoming my caretaker before becoming my wife. Imagine how I felt, not knowing what was in front of me and the possibility of me dying and making her a widow in what should have been the best time of our lives. This was a chance for love for us at this stage of our lives.

There were so many emotions but even though I was afraid I knew somehow; I would get through this.

The second round of bladder cancer proved to be the hardest thing I have ever gone through in my life. They performed two biopsies, rounds, and rounds of chemotherapy and radiation. I experienced cramps throughout my body, my blood pressure was always high and during that time I had to wear embarrassing preventive undergarments. I had to change doctors, change hospitals, and change medications that were giving me terrible effects. I had to advocate for myself from doctors who wanted to continue surgeries. However, regardless of everything I went through, I got through it. By the grace of God, amazing doctors, and my support system, I am cancer free!

I have learned so much from this experience, but one of the main things I have learned is when you experience something of this magnitude your health becomes paramount. As a man I discovered that I did not have a S on my chest and certainly was not invincible.

The first battle with bladder cancer did not scare me much but this time made me rethink my entire life. The very idea that if I had just stayed on top of this it would not have returned as harshly as it did or not at all. Again, I was at my lowest point.

There was a moment within this fight I thought I may not survive and the very idea of not being with my children again because of my poor decisions tortured me. Lying in the hospital with tubes and machines connected to me gave me a different perspective on life. Losing everything I worked so hard for and not being with my Queen helped me make a major decision for my life. I had to make changes quickly and stick with them. My life has changed so much since then. My mission now is to help every man I can emotionally heal and take accountability for their lives and their bodies.

Deep Healing

My belief system has always been very deep. God has something special for me to do in my life. I had not come close to doing it, so I still had life to live. I still had hope for myself. I still had hope that I would finally get my life back on track. I was determined to stop messing up and disappointing myself and my family. I can be transparent with you all like this because I want you to be transparent with yourself.

Being honest with you and being honest with myself makes me a more confident man than ever. I am not any less of a man because I described some of the horrific things that I have gone through. It is imperative that you see hope. It does not matter what you are going through or how you feel, situations and feelings are only moments that are constantly changing. Knowing this allowed me to feel hope for my tomorrow. It helped me understand that even though at that moment where I was bleeding, and in so much pain I was not going to be in this situation anymore. I knew one day I was going to be healthier even if the entire world gave up on me. I could not give up on me.

I was given my father's name and with it came great expectation and responsibility. I am a father of two amazing children and that comes with great expectation and responsibility. I am also a grandfather and a husband, these titles also come with 4 and responsibilities. God has blessed me with four stepchildren, three godchildren and countless young men who I am counseling. I am a son to my mother n law and a brother to my wife's sisters. I have gained more than I have ever expected! There was an inner fight within me for a life I had not lived in yet. I am grateful for that inner fight not to succumb to depression and cancer because all my dreams would have died with me. Everything that I hold dear to my heart I would have disappointed and lost.

This is my story, and I know there are many men out here who have comparable stories different details but similar. I know there are men out here who wish things would just get better. They wish life were a lot less hard to live. But as a man who has had tests and victories in his life, if I had given up and lost hope I would not be where I am right now. When having hope there must be a bigger picture even when you are exhausted from the battles of life. Exhausted from the bills not getting paid and the responsibility of being head of the family along with all the many hats that you wear 24 hours a day. There is hope.

Sometimes men feel overlooked, unappreciated, and taken for granted. We feel as if no one sees us and no one appreciates the work we do. We are often compared to each other and underestimated. At times, we are not considered as human but more like a bot with no emotions, thoughts, or concerns. Sometimes we feel as if we are only good for what we can provide. As if our worth is tied to our pockets, our salary, the car we drive, the clothes we wear and our homes. There is so much more to us than these things but first we must realize that it is not how others view us or validate us but how we measure ourselves.

Your feelings matter. They are valid and should be heard. It is normal to have doubts and fears and even frustration sometimes. But despite what may be presently happening there is still hope for better. Stop buffering over the problems and start using that energy to find a solution. My solution was to begin taking better care of myself. I had to stop taking my physical and mental health for granted because I had too much to live for.

Time for a Reset

Our hope lies within the resetting of our lives. A reset requires us to setup a readjustment from the situation. For example, there are some of us that are trying to finish school and for financial reasons we have not. This is an opportunity for a reset. An opportunity for us to save our money or apply for loans or a grant. This can also be an opportunity to research a second alternative to college. When you are not in school you can choose another major or even conclude school is not for you.

Hope can lie within the end of a relationship. Instead of staying in something that is not working for us, we should let it go and prepare ourselves for the right person.

Sometimes the disappointment and heartache are hope resetting your priorities and value of yourself.

Trust the process of an ending because it could be the dawn of a beginning. Everyone's journey is unique and important. Be patient with yourself and seek those who are understanding and supportive of you. Embrace the concept of hope and give every situation a chance to be better. If necessary, encourage yourself and take the initiative to change your mindset.

Hope is always on the other side of fear. Fear stands in the way of progress. Fight off negative thoughts and persevere past your doubts of a better tomorrow.

The Fight for Hope

Depression can affect individuals from all walks of life. However, it is essential to recognize that there is hope even in the midst of darkness. Let us talk a little more about hope for men fighting depression. Hope is a powerful belief or expectation that things can and will get better. Whatever the situation is it will have a positive expected end. It is a vital force that allows individuals to see beyond their current circumstances and envision a future filled with possibilities. But for men struggling with depression, it may serve as a beacon of light reminding them that their situation is not permanent and that there is a way forward.

Men living with depression often encounter unique challenges when it comes to seeking help and expressing their emotions. One of the most significant aspects of hope for men with depression is a gradual breaking down of the stigma surrounding mental health. As more men come forward to share their experiences, their feeling of seeking help for mental health issues is gradually shifting. By challenging societal norms and encouraging open conversations hope is fostered allowing men to seek help without feeling ashamed or weak.

Building a dedicated support network is crucial for men struggling with depression. Support groups specifically tailored for men with depression can also offer a safe space for sharing experiences and finding solace in the knowledge that they are not alone.

As I have said many times within this book, building a strong support network is crucial for men struggling with depression. Friends, family, and professional resources can provide the necessary encouragement and guidance during these challenging times.

Hope for men with depression lies in the knowledge that effective treatments are available and that recovery is possible. Seek professional help, such as therapy or if needed, medication. Give more concern for your mental well-being and provide yourself with a path to healing. Understand that depression is a treatable condition and that there are success stories of men overcoming this fight. Instill a sense of hope and motivation so that you can persevere.

Hope is a fundamental component in the journey towards overcoming depression for men. It involves recognizing the challenges faced by men struggling with depression and breaking down societal stigmas. Knock down the walls of uncertainty regarding your life. Be honest with yourself concerning your cognitive health. We know before anyone else when we do not feel like ourselves.

The fostering of hope helps men find the strength to navigate their way out of the darkness and embrace a future filled with possibilities. Remember there is life after depression, and no one should face it alone.

Owning Your Journey

The Power of Taking Charge and Making a Change

Chapter 9

Accountability and Responsibility

"Leaders inspire accountability through their ability to accept responsibility."

This may ruffle some feathers, and some may debate this statement, but men are natural born leaders. Whether they accept it or not, it's indeed a fact. We are born and designed to lead. We all have this trait within us. But we can also say that some men should not lead. There are major parts of their character that are attached to unhealed places. It proves that they would be unfit to lead. Some lack accountability and this makes them untrustworthy as a leader. Real leaders take on responsibility for their actions. Whether it feels good or makes us look bad. Nevertheless, they acknowledge their mistakes and make amends when it is necessary.

Prevailing Obstacles

Men have always faced unique challenges when it comes to accountability due to societal expectations, gender norms and cultural restrictions. Traditional masculinity roles are often prioritized as strength, independence, and self-reliance. Because of these restrictions it becomes harder for men to admit when they are vulnerable and when they have shortcomings. It makes it hard for them to confront their issues. But despite their obstacles, men must make accountability a guiding principle for their life, or they will never take responsibility for their actions. They will not produce healthier responses when faced with disappointment.

Though society has its restrictions on us to be, acting and living a certain way we are still responsible for our own actions and our decisions regarding our lives and the people we are connected to. For example, if you borrow money from the bank, you are responsible for paying it back and you must hold yourself accountable for that obligation. The same applies to your emotional health. When a man neglects his mental health, it will have negative consequences on his overall well-being and his quality of life.

Quality of life can be reflected in your health. My personal journey required major determination to be responsible for myself. I was always active and enjoyed working out, traveling, and being with family. Eating well and taking supplements was a big part of my regimen so when I received the diagnosis of bladder cancer I experienced a whirlwind of emotions. It turned my world upside down. I began questioning myself and everything I was sensitive to in my life. I even began searching my family tree to see if it was hereditary. The physical symptoms of this condition challenged my mental health. The pain I experienced and the embarrassment I felt humbled me.

I had plans for my life but suddenly all I could see was cancer. The physical symptoms of this condition began to take a toll on me. The pain and the fatigue caused anxiety. The emotional distress combined with constant doctor visits wherein I endured multiple needles and exams. The embarrassment was overwhelming.

I did not have the privilege of undergoing this experience privately. My soon to be bride had a front row seat to every horrific event that happened. I understood that to fulfill my responsibility to my wife I had to apply it to myself, first. This newfound determination helped me prioritize my life and helped me quickly learn that the self-discipline I needed to become healthy again was needed in every aspect of my life. My journey required a deeper spiritual connection as well as a decrease in my stress load. I made the necessary changes for my life. It was clear to me that stressing over things I had no control over was killing me.

Learning the skill of wearing people like lose clothes was epic for me. Everything was on the line, and I promised myself I would fight for my life and get back on track. Everything else had to take a back seat. This was my step toward better mental health. It was the change in my mindset that gave me the strength to return to my job while enduring rounds of chemo and radiation. The eagerness to marry my Queen, start my business and author this book. God is Good, y'all.

Unaddressed chronic stress can create anxiety and negatively affect a man's physical health. It can cause weakened immune systems, heighten the risk of developing chronic illnesses, and increase unhealthy bingeing on fast foods that basically become coping mechanisms. It can also affect performances within our relationships, such as strains amongst our family and friends and romantic partners. Mental health neglect can impair cognitive function. Your memory, your inability to concentrate and your decision-making abilities. This can change your plans for your future immensely. Increased emotional neglect can have detrimental results by increasing the risk of suicidal thoughts due to the constant feeling of sorrow. Men are particularly more vulnerable to suicide than women because of social expectations and its discouragement towards men seeking help or expressing their emotions. The results of men downplaying their emotions leads to a higher risk of experiencing intense feelings of hopelessness and despair.

Being accountable to ourselves is more than just protecting our masculinity. Our emotional health is just as important. A man's mental state decides his quality of life. Take on the responsibility of completing a self-analysis about your emotional health. Incorporate daily journals of your emotional road map within your regimen. Attaining intelligence in this regard can encourage self-reflection and a greater willingness to take responsibility for one's actions. Your emotional stability should become more important to you day by day. This will aid you by recognizing and understanding your own emotions and empathizing with others.

Our Word is our Bond

When I think of the word accountability, I remember this saying that I learned long ago. A man is only as good as his word. As men when it comes to emotional health and fighting off depression it is imperative that we make a commitment to ourselves. Once the commitment is made, we must follow up with the necessary tools to help us get through it. It is the same as making a commitment to work on our bodies at the gym. In the beginning we commit to a certain number of times of the week to go to the gym. At some point, however, the excitement of going to the gym wears off and that is when the real commitment begins. This is when the real struggle to continue occurs. Your body slows down, and you begin to experience pain from unused muscles. Without a real obligation to your regimen your gym time will begin to decline significantly. I experienced this after cancer. I gained 50 pounds, and it affected everything in my life. I made a commitment to get back into the gym and eat healthy again, but it proved to be harder than I expected. Getting back into my old routine has proven to be more difficult than I expected. Eating healthily before cancer was easier for me than it is now because I was seeking a mental escape from my reality and catered to comfort food.

The same goes for my emotional health. Cancer brought on depression. Yes, guys' sickness for a prolonged period can bring on depression. It can take a toll on your mental and physical capabilities and send you down a rabbit hole. You must be determined to get out of it regardless of how it may seem.

When we are facing difficult challenges, we do not have to fight it all by ourselves. Sometimes we need someone we can trust to be a listening ear and help us remain accountable for the task at hand. I did not have to look too far for an accountability partner. My wife is my partner through life and everything it entails. Having a partner during emotional battles makes it easier to endure. My responsibility to her and our marriage holds me accountable. It is my responsibility to be emotionally healthy and physically fit for her. The normal marriage vows were recited but I added more to mine. I promised to give her my love and to give her the absolute best of me. However, it starts with me. The commitment started with me. Take responsibility for yourself. Develop self-reflection.

Pay attention to the changes in your attitudes and moods. Self-awareness is an ongoing process that takes time to master. It requires a man that is committed to cultivating himself through his personal transformation. Self-analysis is the process examining our thoughts, feelings, and behaviors to gain a deeper understanding of yourself. Mindfulness will help you explore your inner thoughts. Develop self-awareness by paying attention to your patterns, triggers, and habits. Notice how you respond to different situations and find any recurring themes in your life. Ask yourself questions to delve deeper into your thoughts and feelings. For example, why do I feel a certain way in this situation? What underlying beliefs are influencing my behavior?

Identify your patterns. Look for patterns in your thoughts, emotions, and behaviors. Identify patterns that can help you understand your tendencies and make positive changes. Explore your values and beliefs. Examine them and consider how they align with your actions and whether any adjustments are needed. Set goals for yourself based on your analysis. Be sure they are realistic and meaningful for personal growth and development. These goals can help guide your actions and provide a sense of direction. Self-analysis is an ongoing process that requires you to have patience with yourself. It can be helpful to seek guidance from a therapist or counselor if you feel the need for professional support on this journey.

Let us talk more about the importance of learning yourself. A fantastic way of self-reflection is meditation. Meditation can be done anywhere, anytime, alone or with a group of people. It just requires silence. My wife and I have a healthy routine. When we both get home, we greet each other and talk about our day. We talk about business and family and have dinner then she will go to the back of the house, and I will go to the front. I love a quiet dark room where I can relax, think through my day, and focus on some things. She is the opposite of me. She needs white noise. She is a natural born multitasker. She never does one thing at a time. I have watched her in amazement researching on the computer, finishing homework, and on social media on her phone all at the same time. Silence disturbs her normalcy.

In my private time I can check myself and my emotions. There are times when I have had a grueling day, and I would just sit in the car for a while until the day has escaped me. I do this to avoid reliving the drama. I also do it so not to unload on my wife. For our marriage and peace in the home, I would rather brunt the weight but at the same time I must have limits. I must be accountable for my own mental ability. I must measure my emotional capacity with diligence to determine if I have surpassed my limits. We all have signs when something is too much for us to handle. In my case, I quickly become short with people or easily aggravated. I realized at this point I needed to grab my tools and get to work.

A great analogy for taking care of your mental health is, *"just like car batteries, we all need to recharge."* Discover where you hold your emotional baggage. We physically carry our problems in our bodies. We tend to carry our stress differently than women. Because of this the signs of depression are usually considered stealth. Stealth depression signs in men are weight disturbances, agitation, and anger issues. Take notice of these signs like tension in the back or shoulders, grinding your teeth when you sleep or muscle pains.

These symptoms are never connected to emotional stress. Most of us shrug it off and pretend as if everything is fine. Truthfully speaking, cancers, disorders and diseases usually start with symptoms we refuse to check. Thinking that it will only add to our stress. We wonder, why should we dig up something that may or may not be there. We must be accountable for not only our physical health but matters that cause us stress.

Men Stressors

Most major stressors like financial problems play a huge role in our mental health. For a man not to be able to provide for his family or even for himself can send our stress through the roof. As a father and a husband, I am bound to provide for my family. According to society men are judged by their ability to provide. This type of pressure creates an array of emotions. Things do not always work out the way we want them to and when they do not, we feel like failures. We doubt ourselves. We see the disappointing look on our partners faces and we instantly begin to feel guilt. We scramble to improve things and sometimes fall into despair.

Being under intense stress can cause major health problems. I know that the passing of my parents within the same year along with my personal problems, were linked together with my time with cancer. I internalized everything, and it hurt me from the inside out. It nearly claimed my life until I put things in perspective. I had a good long talk with myself in the mirror and promised to take better care of him. I promised to not allow disappointment whether from myself or others to lay stagnant within my mind. I promised to love me better.

Sometimes in these lessons from life you must take the responsibility of self and again. Wear people like loose clothing. You are not always at fault for how things turn out. Do your best and if that does not accomplish what is desired, try again. If the relationship does not work out be accountable for your part in it and move on, especially if it is toxic. If the business deal doesn't work out the way you desired work on the next deal. Study and learn what you need to know to be better the next time. As long as you are breathing you have a chance to do better.

We fight depression because we feel as though we have no choice but to cater to social norms and live in our misery. We fear what someone may say or think of us. We need to get to the position where the only opinion that matters most about us is our own. When this occurs, depression will not stand a chance.

Depression falls upon a man whose opinion of himself is embedded in someone else's idea of him. It usually stems from a harsh response from someone who harbored negative feelings toward you initially.

Too many of us men are dying prematurely because of matters that can be worked through, given more thought, planned better or just forgiven. We are killing ourselves because we refuse to accept that there is life on the other side of the problem. Young men watch older men struggle from lack of forgiveness and coping skills year after year. So instead of imitating them and suffer, they decide to unalive themselves.

Suicide is the leading cause of death for men that are under 50. Most men that are over 50 are living with chronic depression completely unaware. Chronic depression is evident in health issues like heart related issues. It causes strokes, heart attacks, digestive issues like IBS or, like in my case, cancer.

Guys take responsibility for the challenges that contribute to your mental health struggles. This includes the stresses that you know about and the stresses that you do not. Also, they can include work relationship issues, unhealthy habits, or even unresolved emotional issues. Recognizing these challenges could be the first step toward finding solutions and gaining control of your mental health. Acknowledge when you need support and seek it earnestly. Seeking support empowers you.

Addressing your mental health concerns will provide you with the tools you need to regain control over your life. Unfortunately, we are harder on ourselves than anyone else can be. The neglect of having the tools we need to heal can cause us to search for easier attainable vices which can lead to substance abuse or alcohol. Men tend to use more lethal ways when punishing themselves, even when considering suicide. Most suicides by men are done by guns or hangings, therefore their completion rate is higher. We are more prone to this because of underreporting and misdiagnosis of depression. The results of inadequate support and treatment allow men to feel that there is only one way out.

Set boundaries for people and for yourself. Do not allow anyone to push you beyond your emotional and mental limits. If someone in your life causes you to dwell in a dark place emotionally take the courage and be responsible for yourself to get out of that relationship. It also means recognizing what and who drains you of your energy and who/what affects you negatively or toxically. Say no to excessive demands by creating a self-capable team and distance yourself if necessary. Protect your mental health for your own well-being.

It is important to note that responsibility and accountability should not be burdensome or lead you to blame yourself for the action of others. It is, however, necessary for you to recognize your part in the situation. Mental health can be influenced by a lot of factors like genetics, the environment, even life circumstances but only take responsibility for the part you play. You are not responsible for anyone else's choices.

Being responsible and accountable is about recognizing what is within your control and taking steps to support your mental health. If you are struggling remember to seek professional guidance and support from a mental health professional who can provide the necessary care and assistance that you need. Guys, your healing is the utmost importance part of your mental health and only you can make it a priority.

A Journey of Transformation

Embracing New Beginnings and Reclaiming Your Life

Chapter 10

Restart, Renew and Restore

"Hit the reset button. Whatever happened yesterday, forget about it. Get a new perspective.

Today is a new day." Germany Kent

Take the emotional scalpel and remove every assault, heartache, trauma, betrayal, and setback that has manipulated your life from this point and back. They do not belong in your life anymore. Let's start all over. The clean slate begins when you believe that you can do better. It starts small. Little thoughts can form big dreams and goals. Big ideas will cause a motion or a forward movement that first must begin with your mindset.

Have you ever had a problem with your car and instead of lifting the hood and finding the problem you sit behind the wheel and wish it to move. That is not wise, right guys. To restart you must find the problem and resolve it. Starting over means returning to the drawing board. Take the time to think about life beyond that situation. What do you see? Even something as hard as death. Losing someone close to you can be detrimental to emotional health. But if your loved one knew you well, would they want you to live your life free or bound? Would they want you to stay at the grave in a state of mourning or would they want you to enjoy your time as if they were with you.

Life is temporary. Do what needs to be done for your happiness. Do not spend your life buffering over mistakes and situations you have no control over. It is time to restart your life. Your only barrier is yourself and you are the only one stopping you from restarting your life over again. Whether it is an impulsive move or planned event, make the turn for restarting your life by removing the fear. Let us lighten the heaviness of it. Lighten the embarrassment of it. Normalize it and grant yourself some compassion. Once you have given yourself permission to restart and you have addressed your former issues you will discover the road to healing is right at your fingertips. Turn the key to the ignition and hit the gas. Let's go!

Renewing the Mind

Part of the process of restarting is renewing the mind. Start by letting go of the weight of the past. Let go of the emotional connection to regrets, mistakes, and matters of the past. This will take time and consistency. Training a man's mind to renew itself is like accessing a storm's damage. It is our choice to either step out to safety or allow the storm to overtake us. Either way we must look back and assess the damage. How did this storm affect my life, my finances, and my health? In my case, it affected everything. My mind was trapped in a never-ending cycle of self-doubt and self-criticism. It was taking a toll on me. In a state of depression, I went on a drinking binge and convinced myself I could drive home. I lost control of my car and smashed into someone's home.

I got out of the car in shock at what had just happened. Looked around hysterically to see if anyone was injured or killed from my horrible choice. There was no one home and no one was around. As usual God protected me from myself and from hurting others. There are times when we are our worst enemy. This situation was a punch in the gut for me. I could not go any further. The very idea that I could have inflicted someone else because of the feelings that were consuming me. This sickened me. I made a choice to change and let go of everything that made me spiral. I needed time to reflect on my problems and to stop pretending I had the answers because it was clear that I did not. I accepted the past as it was behind me. I was unable to correct any of my bad decisions. All I could do was move forward. Beginning my exodus from the mental prison I put myself in, I began to tear down learnt behavior brought upon by drinking and self-medicating my mental fogs, struggles and self-criticisms. The renewing of my mind was taking place.

Another way of renewing is making a determination never to limit yourself to mistakes or tragedies. Though your mind was stuck there for some time, you continued to work, sleep, eat and engage with others. The trauma manipulated you into staying there.

How does one change his own mind? Usually, it comes from outside forces. Sometimes it can be people encouraging you like family, friends and even support groups. Positive reinforcements can occur from many places that only require an open mind. Allow yourself to hear the words that were once muffled by depression. Take a mental analysis of the voices in your head and their messages. Make one of the hardest decisions you have ever made in your mental health journey. Decide not to listen to the negativity coming from within. Censor your thoughts toward yourself because it always starts with you.

Once you begin to demand positivity inwardly the same will be demanded outwardly.

Be a Better Version of Yourself

I will always be honest and transparent with you all. Conquering depression is no easy task. But allowing it to rob you of life is horrendous. It can be challenging but you are worth the fight. It can feel lonely at times. Prepare for those moments. Invite friends over, attend comedy shows, spend time with your family, play sports, exercise, get away to somewhere fun, meditate, or pray but just do not stay in that state. You have the power to change your feelings.

Feelings are temporary because they change from moment to moment and should not be the source of a permanent decision. By making this mistake, we shortly regret the decision that we are now forced to live with. Search for that man buried under the rubble of past hurt and trauma. Remember what it was like not to be sad, angry all the time, and miserable. The rebirth of you is a day of reckoning. The day when the weight of the past fell to the ground.

Before any gender roles there is humanity. We all have emotions. We all have hurt and pain. We all cry. Part of my restoration was to embrace the vulnerable side of me. I allowed myself to feel sadness and express it, but I learned the necessity of letting it all go. I learned to process my feelings but not allowing a passing feeling to connect with my personality. I cannot allow it to rule my life, my relationships, my career choices, and my health.

I choose to be the light I need and control the dark side of me. This took time to learn, and I am still learning. Learning about self is a lifetime journey. It requires patience with yourself and the ability to dust yourself off when you fall. We are not seeking perfection. Perfection is a fantasy. It is a word we love to throw around, but no one has achieved. We all have a dark side that must be managed and disciplined. Some of us have allowed this side of us to be the decision maker when it comes to our problems. We have also allowed this entity to play judge and jury towards people who were innocent of the hurtful acts done to us. This anger still dwells inside you. Remove it and replace it with peace.

Challenge your old way of thinking by reading books of inspiration and hope. The most powerful tool you have in this journey is your mind. Our thoughts shape who we are and who we choose to be. Repurpose this tool to heal itself and start again. Your mind holds secrets about yourself you have yet to discover. Allow it to awaken from the prison of depression and thrive. Proving to yourself that you can heal from your trauma and be restored. Your validations are internal, and your life can be filled with promise, joy, love, and happiness.

Embracing the Path to a Happy, Depression-Free Life: A Call to Men

In today's fast-paced and demanding world, it is crucial for men to prioritize their mental health and well-being. Depression, a silent but prevalent condition, affects millions of men worldwide. However, by adopting certain strategies and making conscious choices, men can navigate the path towards a happier, depression-free life.

One of the first steps towards a depression-free life is breaking the stigma associated with mental health. Men often face societal expectations to be strong, stoic, and unemotional, which can make it challenging to acknowledge and address their mental health struggles. By challenging these stereotypes and encouraging open discussions, we can create a safe and supportive environment for men to look for and help each other without judgement and shame.

Men should recognize that seeking emotional help will set them on a pathway of freedom. Mental health professionals, such as therapists or counselors, can provide valuable guidance and support in navigating through depression. They offer strategies to cope with stress, manage emotions, and develop healthy coping mechanisms. Seeking therapy can empower men to understand their emotions better and develop effective strategies to combat depression.

Developing a dedicated support system is essential for men to lead a happy and depression-free life. Surrounding oneself with understanding and empathetic individuals, such as friends, family, or a support group, can provide a sense of belonging and reassurance. Having someone to talk to, share experiences with and lean on during challenging times can make a significant difference in one's mental well-being. Engaging in healthy habits can significantly contribute to overall mental health and happiness. Regular exercise, a balanced diet and sufficient sleep are also vital elements in maintaining emotional wellbeing. Physical activity releases endorphins, which act as natural mood boosters. A nutritious diet and quality sleep support brain function and help regulate emotions. By prioritizing these habits, men can reduce the risk of depression and enhance their overall quality of life.

Practicing mindfulness and self-care can help men develop a deeper understanding of their thoughts and emotions. Engaging in activities such as mediation, deep breathing exercises, or journaling can promote self-reflection and emotional awareness. It is time for us to engage more with ourselves and put the energy we put into other things that are important to us into ourselves. Take time, engage in hobbies, and pursue your passions for these are crucial for self-care. When men begin nurturing their own well-being, men can cultivate resilience and find joy in their daily lives.

Obtaining a sense of purpose and deeper meaning in life is essential for happiness and mental well-being. Men can explore their interest, set goals, and pursue meaningful endeavors that align with their values. Engaging in volunteer work or contributing to their communities can provide a sense of fulfillment and purpose. By finding meaning in their lives, men can develop a positive mindset and a keen sense of self-worth.

Stress can often contribute to the development of depression. Men should develop effective stress management techniques because negativity can impact our mental health. Strategies such as time management, setting realistic goals, and practicing relaxation techniques can help reduce stress levels. Engaging in hobbies, spending time in nature, or taking part in activities that bring joy can also serve as effective stress relievers.

Living a happy, depression-free life is a journey that requires self-reflection, courage, and commitment. By breaking the stigma, seeking professional help, building a supportive network, cultivating healthy habits, embracing mindfulness and self-care, the finding of purpose and managing stress, men can take control of their mental wellbeing and lead fulfilling lives.

Let us encourage each other to prioritize our mental health, uplift each other, and create a society of happiness and emotional well-being. Let us create a life full of value and celebrate our new beginning. Remember, every step taken towards a happier life is a step towards a brighter future.

Acknowledgments

I would like to express my heartfelt gratitude to all those who have contributed to the creation of "Men Conquering Depression." This book is not just a reflection of my thoughts and experiences, but a culmination of the support, insights, and encouragement I have received from many incredible individuals along the way.

First and foremost, I want to thank the men who bravely shared their stories with me. Your vulnerability and honesty have inspired me and will undoubtedly inspire countless others. Your willingness to confront your struggles and share your journeys is a testament to your strength and resilience.

I am immensely grateful to my family and friends for their unwavering support. Your belief in me and this project has been a source of motivation, especially during the challenging times of writing. Thank you for listening, encouraging, and cheering me on.

I would also like to acknowledge the mental health professionals and organizations that provided valuable resources and insights. Your dedication to helping others navigate their mental health journeys is both admirable and essential. Thank you for your tireless work and for being a guiding light for those in need.

To my editor and publishing team, your expertise and guidance have been invaluable.

Thank you for your patience, encouragement, and for believing in the importance of this message.

Lastly, I would like to thank everyone who has ever struggled with depression or has supported someone who has. Your strength is remarkable, and together, we can continue to break the stigma and foster understanding around mental health.

This book is dedicated to all of you who are on the path to conquering your struggles. May we continue to find hope, healing, and strength in each other.

With gratitude,

Fred

Epilogue

The book "Men Conquering Depression" provides valuable guidance and support to men struggling with depression. Here is how the author addresses each of the chapters:

Chapter 1 "Coming out of the Darkness": This chapter focuses on helping men recognize and acknowledge their depressive feelings and experiences. It provides strategies and encouragement for men to confront their emotions, seek help and begin their journey.

Chapter 2 "Get Out and Get Help": This chapter emphasizes the importance of seeking professional help and supportive networks. It guides men on how to overcome the barriers to seeking help, such as stigma and self-reliance, and provides resources and strategies for finding proper mental health professionals.

Chapter 3 "The Stress of it All": This chapter explores the impact of stress on mental health and offers coping mechanisms to manage stress more effectively. It helps men understand the connection between stress and depression and offers practical strategies to reduce and manage stressors in their lives.

Chapter 4 "Removing a failure mindset": This chapter addresses the negative thought patterns and beliefs that often go with depression. It helps men challenge and reframe their feeling of failure, promoting self-compassion and resilience.

Chapter 5 "When there's a chink in my armor": This chapter acknowledges the moments of vulnerability and weakness that men may experience during their depression journey. It provides strategies for self-care, building resilience, and seeking support during these challenging times.

Chapter 6 "Going from Brokenness to Wholeness": This chapter focuses on the process of healing and rebuilding one's sense of self. It offers guidance on self-reflection, self-acceptance, and self-discovery, promoting personal growth and transformation.

Chapter 7 "Removing Shame and Guilt": This chapter addresses the common feelings of shame and guilt that men may experience due to their depression. It provides strategies for letting go of self-blame and cultivating self-compassion and forgiveness.

Chapter 8 "There is Hope": This chapter instills hope and optimism in men by sharing the author's personal story of his fight for hope, recovery, and resilience. It emphasizes that depression is treatable and that there is a brighter future ahead.

Chapter 9 "Accountability and Responsibility": This chapter encourages men to take ownership of their mental health and well-being. It promotes accountability for self-care practices, treatment adherence, and seeking ongoing support.

Chapter 10 "Restart, Renew and Restore": This chapter focuses on rebuilding a fulfilling and balanced life after depression. It offers guidance on setting goals, nurturing relationships, and maintaining mental health practices to sustain long-term well-being.

Men Conquering Depression provides practical strategies, personal stories, and resources to empower men in their journey to conquer depression and reclaim their lives. It addresses various aspects of the depressive experience and offers guidance on seeking help, managing stress, changing negative thought patterns, and fostering personal growth and healing.

Appendix

Resources for Men Conquering Depression

This appendix provides a comprehensive list of resources that can complement and support the content discussed in the book "Men Conquering Depression." These resources aim to provide additional guidance, tools, and support for men who are navigating their journey towards conquering depression. The following resources cover various aspects of mental health, therapy, self-help, and community support.

1. National Suicide Prevention Lifeline:

- Website: [suicidepreventionlifeline.org] (https://suicidepreventionlifeline.org/)

- Phone: 1-800-273-TALK (1-800-273-8255)

2. Mental Health America:

- Website: [mentalhealthamerica.net] (https://www.mentalhealthameric a.net/)

- Offers educational resources, screening tools, and information on mental health conditions.

3. National Alliance on Mental Illness (NAMI):

- Website: [nami.org] (https://www.nami.org/)

- Provides support, education, and advocacy for individuals and families affected by mental health conditions.

4. Online Therapy Platforms:

- BetterHelp: [betterhelp.com] (https://www.betterhelp.com/)

- Talkspace: [talkspace.com] (https://www.talkspace.com/)

- Offers convenient and accessible online therapy options for individuals seeking professional help.

5. Books and Literature:

- "The Depression Cure" by Stephen S. Ilardi

- "Lost Connections: Uncovering the Real Causes of Depression – and the Unexpected Solutions" by Johann Hari

- "The Upward Spiral: Using Neuroscience to Reverse the Course of Depression, One Small Change at a Time" by Alex Korb

- "The Mindful Way through Depression: Freeing Yourself from Chronic Unhappiness" by Mark Williams, John Teasdale, Zindel Segal, and Jon Kabat-Zinn

6. Support Groups and Online Communities:

- Meetup: [meetup.com] (https://www.meetup.com/)

- Depression and Bipolar Support Alliance (DBSA): [dbsalliance.org] (https://www.dbsalliance.org/)

7. Meditation and Mindfulness Apps:

- Headspace: [headspace.com] (https://www.headspace.com/)

- Calm: [calm.com] (https://www.calm.com/)

8. Exercise and Physical Health:

 - American Psychological Association - Exercise and Mental Health: [apa.org] (https://www.apa.org/monitor/2011/12/exercise)

Please note that this is not an exhaustive list, and it is recommended to explore additional resources and consult with mental health professionals to tailor the support to individual needs. Remember, seeking help and support is an essential step towards conquering depression and achieving overall well-being.

Author's Bio

Fred Majette is an accomplished author and mental health advocate who has dedicated his life to helping men conquer depression. With a deep understanding of the challenges faced by men in their mental health journey, Fred's work focuses on empowering individuals to overcome the stigma surrounding depression and seek the support they need.

Having experienced his own battle with depression, Fred's personal journey inspired him to share his insights and strategies for navigating the often-misunderstood world of mental health. Through his book, "Men Conquering Depression," Fred provides a compassionate and practical guide that offers meaningful tools and resources for men looking to regain control of their lives.

Fred's writing is characterized by his empathetic approach, combining personal anecdotes with evidence-based research to create a relatable and informative narrative. His work emphasizes the importance of self-care, therapy, and community support in overcoming depression. By sharing his own experiences and the stories of others, Fred aims to break down the barriers that prevent men from seeking help and foster a culture of mental health awareness and acceptance.

In addition to his writing, Fred actively engages with mental health organizations, speaking at conferences, broadcasts his weekly podcast MCD podcast and one on one counseling for men to promote mental well-being and encourage open conversations about depression. Through his work, Fred continues to inspire and empower men to confront their mental health challenges and find a path towards healing and resilience.

Fred Majette's book, "Men Conquering Depression," is a testament to his commitment to improving the lives of individuals struggling with mental health issues. With compassion, knowledge, and a genuine desire to make a difference, Fred's work serves as a guiding light for those seeking hope and transformation in their journey towards conquering depression.

Fred Majette, an exceptional author, visionary entrepreneur, and mental health advocate. As the founder and CEO of Visionary Concepts Corporation, Fred has built a reputation for innovative thinking and challenging the status quo. With a motto that embodies his philosophy - "Say what they aren't saying, write what they aren't writing, and create what they aren't creating" - Fred has established himself as a trailblazer in multiple industries.

Beyond his literary accomplishments, Fred has extended his expertise into the world of natural skincare and haircare. Through his companies Ze' ne Fari and Beards Balm and Brawn, he has revolutionized the way men care for their skin and hair, offering products that are both effective and sustainable. With a focus on using natural ingredients and promoting self-care, Fred's brands have garnered a loyal following and have become synonymous with quality and authenticity.

In addition to his entrepreneurial ventures, Fred has developed a companion workbook for his groundbreaking book, "Men Conquering Depression." This workbook provides readers with practical exercises and tools to facilitate their journey towards healing and resilience. By combining his individual experiences with evidence-based strategies, Fred empowers his readers to take control of their mental health and embrace a brighter future.

Fred's passion for spreading mental health awareness extends beyond the pages of his book. He hosts the MCD podcast, where he engages in candid conversations with experts and individuals who have triumphed over depression. Through this platform, Fred seeks to break down the stigma surrounding mental health and inspire others to seek support and share their stories.

To further empower his audience, Fred has also launched his clothing line, Beau & Bella. With a focus on promoting self-expression and confidence, the brand offers stylish apparel that encourages individuals to embrace their uniqueness and celebrate their journey towards mental well-being.

Fred Majette's accomplishments as an author, visionary entrepreneur, and mental health advocate are truly remarkable. Through his innovative thinking, commitment to self-care, and dedication to empowering others, Fred has made a lasting impact on countless lives.

Join Fred on this transformative journey and discover the power within you to conquer depression and embrace a life of resilience and fulfillment.

Made in the USA
Middletown, DE
01 November 2024